Table of Contents

Introduction

Unit One

Lesson 1

Lesson 2

Unit Two

Lesson 3

Lesson 4

Unit Three

Lesson 5

Phonetic Code Used in this Book

It is necessary to refer to individual speech sounds, technically referred to as *phonemes*, throughout the manual. In order to do so as clearly as possible, the following code is used. The code was selected to make learning it as easy as possible. For the most part each phoneme is represented by a common spelling for the sound.

at	day	new	rip
Ed	see	cook	rib
it	pie	saw	fit
odd	boat	cow	lid
up	cue	toy	look
her	car	or	pig
if	wish	sing	
vet	zh (beige)	hat	
thin	much	wet	
dh (that)	jug	yes	
gas	ham	lip	
zoo	can	rip	

The underlined part of the words in the table above represents the code for the sound that letter represents in the word. For instance, the so-called long-i sound is represented by the letters *ie*, as in the word *pie*.

Throughout this book I will indicate phonemes using the symbols in the above chart between forward slashes, e.g., /a/, /sh, /ee/. Thus, I will show the sounds of the word *catch* as /k/ /a/ /ch/.

The technical term for the letter or letters used to represent a phoneme is *grapheme*. I do use this term occasionally, but I use as much as possible the less technical term, *spelling* instead so long as the meaning of the sentence remains clear. I will present graphemes/spellings in italics. Thus, some of the graphemes or spellings for the sound /oa/ are *oa*, *oe*, *ow*, *o*, and *o-e*.

There are two sounds that are represented in this code by non-standard graphemes. The code *dh* is used to represent the phoneme at the beginning of the word *that*. There is only one grapheme used in English to represent this sound, namely *th*, but this also happens to be the only grapheme used to represent the sound at the beginning of the word *thin*.

The code *zh* is used to represent the last phoneme in the word *beige*. This phoneme occurs in a few one-syllable loan words from French such as *beige* and *rouge*, in some words with *su*, such as *measure*, and *casual*, and in the *sion* syllable in words such as *vision* and *fusion*. I've included it so that I have a complete code for all of the sounds of English, but you won't have to worry about it because no words with this sound are part of the material you will cover in this book.

Note about the use of *he* and *she*

There is no way to use a generic third person singular pronoun in English without being either clunky or sexist. One can be elegant but sexist and use "he," or non-sexist but somewhat forced and use "she." I have chosen to address this conundrum by splitting the difference, as it were, and using "he" in the introductory chapters, and "she" in the lesson text. This solution may be diplomatic or it may be cowadly, I'm still not sure, but it was easy enough to implement, and if I offend any readers on this score, I at least do not do so throughout the entire book.

Introduction

ABeCeDarian Level B2 is a completion of the phonics and word study work begun in Level B1 and will bring a student to a second-grade reading level. To teach Level B2 well, the teacher must be familiar with all of the material presented in Teacher Manual B1.

The phonics covered in B2 can be divided into 3 main sections:

1. a continuation of the work in B1 in which students sort the different ways to spell a sound

2. new work involving flexing the one-letter vowel spellings a, e, i, o, and u in two-syllable words

3. sorting four common vowel spellings according to the multiple sounds each can represent

Sorting different ways to spell a sound

In Units 1 and 2 students sort, respectively, the ways to spell the sounds /s/ and /j/. These are the only consonant sounds sorted in ABeCeDarian. They are presented because they are the consonant sounds that have the most variations (there are 5 common ways to spell /s/ and 4 common ways to spell /j/) and these spellings appear in a very large number of common words.

When "c" is /s/

One of the spellings for /s/ that students sort in this section receives special attention, namely, the letter c. This letter can be used to represent not only the /s/ sound, but also the /k/ sound. In general when a spelling in English can represent more than one sound, there is no special pattern that governs which sound it represents in a particular word. The letter c, however, is an exception. It's use is governed by a very strong pattern. When the letter is followed by e, i, or y, it almost always represents the sound /s/, and when it is followed by any other letter, it almost always represents the sound /k/.[1] A subpattern that students will also learn is to that ce can represent the two separate sounds /s/ + /e/ as in cent and excel, as well as just the /s/ sound alone when it is found at the end of words, such as in force and ounce. In Unit 1, students learn the three patterns where c is usually /s/, (ce, ci, cy), and then play I Spy with words containing c in which they have to look specifically for the ce, ci, cy pattern. This I Spy exercise is repeated in several subsequent units, as you help your child memorize this pattern and apply it accuarately and rapidly.

Variant spellings for /e/, /i/, and /o/

The so-called short vowel sounds /e/, /i/, and /o/, have one primary spelling each, e, i, and o, respectively. Children learn the primary spellings for these sounds early in ABeCeDarian Level A. Each of these sounds, however, has one or two alternate spellings that appear in a number of common words that second graders need to be able to read.

---

[1]   There are only a handful of exceptions to this pattern, including *soccer, macintosh, Caesar,* and *coelacanth.*

The /e/ sound is often spelled *ea*, as in the words *bread, ready,* and *breath.* Extremely rare spellings of /e/ are also found in the common words, *said, friend, any, many,* and *says.*

The /o/ sound is often spelled with the letter *a* when following a *w*, as in the words *swap, watch, wasp, waffle,* and *swamp.*

The /i/ sound is sometimes spelled with the letter *y*, as in the words *gym, myth, Egypt,* and *system.* A rare spelling of /i/ is found in the word *pretty.*

These sounds are sorted in Units 3, 4, and 6.

Ways to spell /ue/

Students sort the /ue/ sound in Unit 5. (The first sound of the word *unit*, by the way, is the /ue/ sound.) This is technically two sound /y/ and /ew/, but English provides several vowel spellings to represent it in some words and so often treats it as a single sound. Specifically, the /ue/ sound can be represented by the *u-e* in *cube*, the *u* in *music*, the *ue* in *argue*, and the *ew* in *few*. This sound is the only new vowel sound presented in Level B2; all the other vowel sounds have been presented earlier in Levels A1, A2, and B1.

Flexing "a," "e," "i," "o," and "u" in two-syllable words

The work in Units 1-5 that I've just described is organized around a particular sound and students learn several ways to spell that sound. The presentation, in other words, proceeds from *sound* to *spelling*.

The remaining units in B2, in contrast, are organized around a single spelling and present students with the different sounds that the spelling is used to represent. In other words, these remaining units proceed from *spelling* to *sound*.

The letters *a, e, i, o,* and *u*, for instance, each represent 2 common sounds (actually, 3 in the case of the letter *u*), a so-called short sound and a long sound. (Please, by the way, DO NOT use the terms short and long vowel sound when teaching ABeCeDarian. I use them hear solely for reference to adult readers who may already be familiar with the terms.) When reading an unfamiliar longer word with one of these letters, it is often not possible for the reader to know in advance which sound the letter is representing. A wonderful example of this ambiguity can be found in the words *polish* and *Polish*, which have identical spellings but different pronunciations. Specifically, in one word the letter *o* represents /o/ and in the other, /oa/. Many other examples exist in which a similar pattern of letters is pronounced with different vowel sounds in different words, as in *finish* and *final, nature* and *natural, metal* and *meter*.

An efficient technique for dealing with this ambiguity is to *flex* the letter, a technique that students were introduced to in Level B1. *Flexing* means that the reader will try one sound. If that doesn't yield a sensible word, then he must try the other sound. Flexing is generally a very easy technique to each because many students often adopt it on their own without formal instruction. To help students become automatic at flexing these letters, they will do very brief exercises in which they read short nonsense syllables and have to read them two ways, once with one vowel sound and then the other. Students are taught to begin their flexing with /a/, /e/, /i/, /o/, or /u/ (that is, the so-called short sound), as this will yield the correct result slightly more than half of the time.

Flexing "ea," "ou," "ar," and "ough"

The final units of Level B2 focus on exposing students to the multiple common sounds that *ea, ou, ar,* and *ough* represent.

The *ea* can represent the sounds /ee/, /e/, and /ay/ as in the words *eat, bread,* and *steak.*

The *ou* can represent the sounds /ow/, /ew/, and /u/ as in *mouth, soup, double.* (The *ou* can also represent the sound /oa/ as in *soul* and *shoulder,* but these words aren't included in this book because they are above the second grade level.)

The letters *ar* can represent /ar/ /or/, /a/ + /r/, and /ay/ + /r/ as in *car, dollar, carrot,* and *care.*

And, arguably the most confusing and difficult spelling in English, *ough,* can represent /ow/, /ew/, /ow/, /aw/, /u/ + /f/, and /aw/ + f, as in *though, through, drought, brought, enough,* and *cough.*

Other Letter/Sound Patterns Presented in B2

In addition to these main patterns, students explore several other advanced letter/sound patterns.

VC and VCe

In Level B1, students are introduced to the spellings *a-e, e-e, i-e, o-e,* and *u-e,* representing the sounds, respectively, /ay/, /ee/, /ie/, /oa/, and /ew/, as in the words, *tape, these, like, note,* and *flute.* In many units of B2 words with these spellings are among the target words to learn in a unit, paired with a word with the same letters minus the final *e.* These pairs include *take/tack, lake/lack, back/bake, snack/snake, lick/like, not/note, hop/hope,* and *can/cane.* (As you can see, the /k/ sound is spelled *ck* in /ak/ and /ik/ and just *k* in /ayk/ and /iek/.)

ph

The spelling *ph* for the /f/ sound is presented in the words *graph* and *phone.*

Silent "h"

The silent *h* in *honest* and *hour* is also presented among the target words. This is one of the few times in ABeCeDarian that a spelling is identified as *silent.*

-tion and -ture

Students learn how to pronounce the endings *tion* and *ture* as in *action* and *nature.*

y + s = ies

Students get the opportunity to read many words formed from a base word ending in *y* to which *s* has been added, such as *carries* and *tries.* These words are presented and practiced in a way very similar to how words with the past tense ended *-ed* are presented in Level B1. Students

also practice reading *does* and *goes*, common words that also have *es* added to a base word rather than just plain *s*.

Additonal material covered

Multisyllable Words

Students receive ample practice reading 2-syllable words in Units 1-8, and, from Unit 9-14, they get practice reading 2, 3, and 4 syllable words.

Commonly Confused Words

The commonly confused pairs *for* and *from*, *what* and *that*, and *come* and *came* are also presented as target words. It is helpful to practice reading these pairs in close proximity to help children read them accurately and quickly.

Supplemental Materials

Check the Support Materials page of the ABeCeDarian website (*www.abcdrp.com/support.asp*) for freely downloadable supplemental materials to use with your child.

Final Comments about Level B2

Students can complete Level B2 in about 6 weeks if they work on it for 20 minutes a day, five days a week. As I mentioned at the beginning of the introduction, students who complete Level B2 will be reading at a 2nd grade level.

Level B2 provides outstanding and efficient phonics and word study instruction for students ready to read at a second grade level. For the full benefit of this instruction, students will also need to do daily oral reading practice for 15-30 minutes on appropriate material as well as 15-30 minutes of appropriate silent reading. It remains extremely beneficial, as well, to continue reading out loud to your child until middle-school age because until then, most children will have oral vocabularies much higher than their reading vocabularies, and so by reading to your child, you can expose him to material with more complicated concepts and language that he will understand and enjoy than he can read on his own. And, of course, reading aloud is just an enjoyable and wonderful way for a family to spend some time together.

The QuickReads series published by Pearson Learning is an excellent resource. Students in ABeCeDarian Level B2 should work in the QuickReads Levels A and B. There are also many trade books suitable for this purpose. One excellent choice is the books that are part of the Random House Step Into Reading series. By the time a student is in the second half of ABeCeDarian B2, he should be able to read the Step Into Reading Step 3 books.

ABeCeDarian Level B2, like the earlier ABeCeDarian materials, is devoted primarily to decoding instruction, that is, instruction designed to help a reader unlock the code and translate print into words. For complete language arts instruction, a child will also need suitable work in comprehension, spelling, and writing.

Summary of Activities in Level B-2

- Sorting Words with the Multiple Spellings of One Sound
- Sorting Words with a Spelling That Represents More Than One Sound
- Reading Multisyllable Words
- I Spy
- Flexing
- Breaking Words Apart
- Completing Fill-in-the-Blank Sentences

Summary of Content in Level B-2

- Spellings for /s/ and /j/ (including *ce, ci, cy* pattern)
- Spellings for /e/, /o/, /i/, and /ue/
- Flexing *a, e, i, o, u, ea, ou, ar, ough*
- *ph*, silent *h*, *y* + *s* = *ies*
- *VC* and *VCe* words
- Easily confused words
- Multi-syllable words

Summary of Content in Level B-2

Unit 1: face, place, nice, mice, twice, twin, twelve, two
(active, include, Easter, demand, hardly, money)

Unit 2: age, page, edge, judge, large, change, giant, bridge
(respect, question, success, power, private, object)

Unit 3: breath, bread, head, ready, take, tack, lake, lack
(direct, wooden, person, final, decide, wonder)

Unit 4: swallow, wash, want, watch, back, bake, snack, snake
(common, pattern, battle, figure, slightly, council)

Unit 5: use, used, cute, few, huge, ever, even, every
(action, capture, station, section, nature, picture)

Unit 6: gym, myth, pretty, of, from, for, come, came
(against, fraction, season, creature, carries, motion)

Unit 7: table, crazy, battle, travel, lick, like, not, note

Unit 8: secret, second, lemon, legal, spies, tries, hurries, puppies

Unit 9: visit, silent, giant, lion, hop, hope, can, cane
(remember, principal, beyond, discover, breakfast, nobody, operation, important)

Unit 10: progress, program, project, broken, does, goes, what, that
(similar, successful, explain, interesting, continue, careful, everything, difference)

Unit 11: student, study, punish, music, hour, honest, phone, graph
(understanding, information, largest, different, kangaroo, however, underneath, machine)

Unit 12: least, scream, bread, deaf, great, break, wear, bear
(operation, telephone, surprise, anything, movement, education, national, company)

Unit 13: mouth, bounce, about, soup, group, youth, young, trouble

Unit 14: shark, darling, carrot, parent, popular, regular, square, area

Unit 15: though, through, drought, brought, enough, thought, dough, cough

s ss c se ce

Unit One

1

Lesson 1

In this lesson your child will:

- sort ways to spell the /s/ sound
- learn the *ce, ci, cy* pattern
- write and analyze 8 high frequency words with the /s/ sound

Sorting Words with s ss c se ce

Have your child open her workbook to pages 4 and 5.

Today you will be reading words that have the /s/ sound.

NOTE: You are saying a SOUND, not letter names.

Please say /s/.

Your child repeats the sound.

Point to the column headings on page 5.

There are five different ways to spell this sound. You're going to sort how the /s/ sound is spelled.

NOTE: There is no need to spell these column headings out loud or to ask your child to do so. She will be paying attention to the specific letters as she performs the activity.

1 s	2 ss	3 c	4 se	5 ce

Please read the first word.

Point to the word *rinse* on page 4 of the student workbook.

NOTE: It's fine if your child recognizes the whole word and calls it out without saying the individual sounds first.

Nice job. Now find which column we should put this word in. Where do you see the match for how /s/ is spelled?

Your child should indicate that the word goes in column 4.

That's right. Please say-and-write __rinse__ in column 4.

Your child should say the sounds in the word one at a time. Each time she says a sound, she should write how it is spelled.

Repeat these steps for the remaining words:

1. Your child reads the word.

2. She indicates in which column the word goes.

3. She records the word in the appropriate column on her sorting sheet. When she records the word, she should say each sound in the word in isolation as she writes how that sound is spelled.

The figure below shows what the completed sorting sheet should look like.

1 s	2 ss	3 c	4 se	5 ce
some	miss	cent	rinse	since
since	boss	city	goose	fence
	press	fancy		force

NOTE: The word since should be recorded in both columns 1 and 5 because it has two /s/ sounds, each spelled a different way.

Reading Words with ce, ci, and cy

When working in Workbook B1, students learned that a single spelling such as *ow* can be used to represent more than one sound. The strategy they have been taught to deal with this variation is to *flex*, that is to try one sound to see if that makes sense; if that sound doesn't yield a word that makes sense, students are to try another sound for the spelling.

The letter *c* can be two sounds commonly, /k/ and /s/. There is no need to flex, however, because there is a very strong pattern that identifies which sound the letter is being used for. This activity introduces students to this pattern. The material in this lesson will be reviewed in subsequent lessons.

Have your child turn to page 6 of her workbook.

Point to the letter *c* at the top of the page.

This letter has 2 main sounds. What are they?

Your child says /k/ and /s/.

NOTE: If your child doesn't know the two sounds, you should say them and have your child repeat.

You've been taught to __flex__ the sounds when you are trying to figure out how to pronounce a spelling that is used for more than one sound. But with this letter, you don't need to flex.

Point to *ce, ci,* and *cy* at the top of the page.

When a word has one of these patterns, then then the <u>cee</u> is /s/. If a word doesn't have this pattern, then the <u>cee</u> is /k/.

Take a good look at the three patterns I have up here. In a second I'm going to cover them up and have you write them down.

Give your child a moment to look at the three patterns and say them. (She should spell them out, i.e., "*cee-ee, cee- i, cee-wy*.")Then cover up the page.

Please write the three patterns I just showed you.

Give your child time to write the patterns on a dry erase board or a separate piece of paper. Then uncover the page so your child can see if she wrote the patterns correctly. If she didn't, have her recite the three patterns once more, then cover up the patterns and have her try to write them from memory again.

After your child can write the 3 patterns correctly from memory, have her read the list of words on the page.

Here are some words with cee-ee, cee-i, and cee-y. Please read them.

Point out to your child that when the *ce* comes at the end of a word, as in the case of *fence*, the *ce* together represents /s/, that is, the *e* does not represent a sound on its own.

I Spy

Have your child turn to page 7 of her workbook.

Now you get to play a game of I Spy. Underline any word that has ce, ci, or cy.

Your child goes through the list underlining any words with ce, ci, or cy.

Please read all of the words. Remember, if you've underlined a word, it fits our pattern and will have a /s/ sound.

Have your child read the words. Repeat as necessay until she can read all of the words accurately without much hesitation.

Breaking Words Apart

Have your child turn to page 8 of her workbook.

Here is another list of words to practice. Please read the first word and then copy it in your workbook.

Your child reads the word and copies it.

You should write the word also on a dry erase board so that you can model the markings she is about to do.

Nice work. Now say each sound in the word and underline how it is spelled.

Your child says the sounds of the word one at a time and underlines how it is spelled. (See the following figure to see how the words should be marked.)

Repeat these steps for the remaining words:

1. Your child reads the word.

2. Your child copies the word neatly in her workbook.

3. Your child says the sounds of the word one at a time. As she says a sound, she underlines how that sound is spelled.

If your child is ever confused about how a particular sound is spelled, tell your child very directly.

<u>Notes about words</u>

Two: Point out to your child that *two* begins with the same letters as *twice, twin,* and *twelve.* Have your child define each of these words, each time eliciting how it is connected to the concept of "2," (*twice* means two times, *twin* means two of the same thing, *twelve* means 10 + 2). Then have your child try to pronounce *two* with the /w/ sound, and point out how difficult it is to say. This is why people don't say the /w/ sound, but keep the letter in the word when writing it.

Tell your child NOT to underline the *w* in *two* when marking the word.

The following figure shows the correct markings for the words.

1. f a c e		5. t w i c e	
2. p l a c e		6. t w i n	
3. n i c e		7. t w e l ve	
4. m i c e		8. t w o	

NOTE: Your child should write the words with normal spacing between the letters. The spacing between the graphemes in the figure above has been exaggerated to make it easy to see the underlines.

Lesson 2

In this lesson your child will:

- practice reading the words she analyzed in the last lesson
- read some two-syllable words
- complete some sentences with the target words in the unit

Word Reading Practice

Have your child turn to page 9 of the student workbook.

nice	two	mice	place	face	twice	twin	twelve
two	twelve	place	twin	nice	face	twice	mice
place	face	twice	nice	mice	twelve	two	twin
mice	twice	twin	face	nice	two	twelve	place

Here are the words you just wrote. Each row has the same words but in a different order. Please read all of the words as well as you can.

Your child reads the words going across each row. You may wish to place a card under the line she is reading to help her keep her place.

Correct any errors immediately.

Reading Two-Syllable Words

Have your child turn to page 10 of her workbook.

1.	active	4.	demand
2.	include	5.	hardly
3.	Easter	6.	money

Here is a list of words with two beats or syllables. When you practiced reading two-syllable words before, you wrote each syllable on a notecard. Now that you're in your new workbook, you'll practice these words in a little different way. I'll do the first one.

I'm going to put a line under each syllable and say it, and then I'll say the whole word.

Put a line under *ac* and pronounce the syllable.

Put a line under *tive* and pronounce the syllable.

Then say the whole word.

Have your child repeat the word.

Please read the rest of the words in this way. Underline each syllable and say it. Then say the whole word.

Your child follows these steps for the remaining words:

1. She underlines the first syllable and says it.

2. She underlines the second syllable and says it.

3. She says the whole word.

> *NOTE: Keep in mind that the point of this exercise is to train students to look at every letter in a multisyllable word in a systematic way. The goal is NOT to teach syllablication rules. For this reason, there will often be more than one acceptable way to identify the syllables. The only requirements are that what your child underlines must be exactly one syllable and easy to say.*

Additional practice

Have your child continue to practice these words in subsequent lessons until she can read them easily. It is fine for her to read the whole word for practice without reading the parts. However, if she has difficulties with a word, she should read it one syllable at a time before saying the whole word.

If your child is good at reading the individual syllables but has problems blending the syllables into whole words,

you should do an oral blending warm-up before a practice session. To conduct the oral blending practice, say the syllables one at a time with a 1 second pause in between and have your child say the whole word. This should be an exclusively oral activity. That is, do not have your child look at the written words when doing this, but just respond to the syllables you say.

Completing Sentences

Have your child turn to page 11 of her workbook.

Here is the page with some sentences for you to complete. Fill in the blank with the choice that makes the most sense.

Remember to say blank when you come to the blank line.

Your child should read the first sentence, saying blank when she comes to the blank line.

Your child should select the word below the blank line that makes the most sense and say-and-write it on the blank line.

Have your child proceed in this way with the remaining sentences. The sentences continue on page 12.

> *NOTE: If your child has great difficulty with handwriting, it's fine for you yourself to write the words on the blank lines. If you do so, however, make sure that your child dictates the sounds of the word to you one at a time.*

The completed sentences should look like the following figure.

1.	Some <u>mice</u> ate the oatmeal in the pantry.
2.	Sam has <u>two</u> sisters.
3.	I went on the roller-coaster <u>twice</u>.
4.	Tom had a big smile on his <u>face</u>.
5.	We had to begin our work at <u>two</u> o'clock.
6.	We had a <u>nice</u> time at Sam's party.
7.	We found <u>twelve</u> mice in the barn.
8.	Please <u>place</u> your books in your desk.
9.	Tom got some sunburn on his <u>face</u>.
10.	I've been to that movie <u>twice</u>.

Unit Checkouts

Before moving on to the next unit, your child should be able to do the following accurately and without much hesitation:

1. Read the 8 target words in the unit easily.

2. Read the two-syllable words in the unit easily.

3. Read the sentences presented in the *Completing Sentences* fluently with virtually 100% accuracy.

j g ge dge

Unit Two

2

Lesson 3

In this lesson your child will:

- sort ways to spell the /j/ sound
- analyze 8 high frequency words with the /j/ sound

Sorting Words with j g ge dge

Have your child open her workbook to pages 14 and 15.

Today you will be reading words that have the /j/ sound.

NOTE: You are saying a SOUND, not a letter name.

Please say /j/.

Your child repeats the sound.

Point to the column headings on page 15.

There are four different ways to spell this sound. You're going to sort how the /j/ sound is spelled.

NOTE: There is no need to spell these column headings out loud or to ask your child to do so. She will be paying attention to the specific letters as she performs the activity.

1 j	2 g	3 ge	4 dge

Please read the first word.

Point to the word *page* on page 14.

NOTE: It's fine if your child recognizes the whole word and calls it out without saying the individual sounds first.

Nice job. Now find which column we should put this word in. Where do you see the match for how /j/ is spelled?

Your child should indicate that the word goes in column 1.

That's right. Please say-and-write page in column 2.

Your child should say the sounds in the word one at a time. Each time she says a sound, she should write how it is spelled.

NOTE: It is also correct to treat the final ge in page (as well as age) as a grapheme and so place them in column 3.

Repeat these steps for the remaining words:

1. Your child reads the word.

2. She indicates in which column the word goes.

3. She records the word in the appropriate column on her sorting sheet. When she records the word, she should say each sound in the word in isolation as she writes how that sound is spelled.

The figure below shows what the completed sorting sheet should look like.

NOTE: The spelling dge represents the /j/ sound. There is no separate /d/ sound in words with this spelling.

1 j	2 g	3 ge	4 dge
jump	page	change	bridge
just	gym	large	badge
	age	George	
	general	charge	

VARIATIONS: Instead of having your child write the words on a sorting sheet, you may wish to write the sorting words on separate note cards and have your child sort the cards. If you do so, make sure to write the words with the spacing used for the words on page 14 of the student workbook. You should also write the column headings *j, g, ge,* and *dge* on separate cards to help your child sort. This variation allows you to reduce the amount that your child has to write. You may also choose to use the sorting sheet but record each word yourself after your child has read it and indicated in which column it should go.

Breaking Words Apart

Have your child turn to page 16 of her workbook.

Here is another list of words to practice. Please read the first word and then copy it in your workbook.

Your child reads the word and copies it on the line underneath the word.

Nice work. Now say each sound in the word and underline how it is spelled.

Repeat these steps for the remaining words:

1. Your child reads the word.

2. She copies the word neatly in her workbook.

3. She says the sounds of the word one at a time. As she says a sound, she underlines how that sound is spelled.

If your child is ever confused about how a particular sound is spelled, tell her very directly.

NOTE: The word giant has two syllables. When your child records this word, she should say the word in syllables and write each syllable on a separate line.

The following figure shows the correct markings for the words.

1.	a g e	5.	l ar ge
2.	p a ge	6.	ch a n ge
3.	e dge	7.	gi a n t
4.	ju dge	8.	b r i dge

NOTE: Your child should write the words with normal spacing between the letters. The spacing between the graphemes in the figure above has been exaggerated to make it easy to see the underlines.

Lesson 4

In this lesson your child will:

- practice reading the words she analyzed in the last lesson
- read some two-syllable words
- complete sentences with the target words in the unit

Word Reading Practice

Have your child turn to page 17 of her workbook.

edge	giant	judge	page	age	large	change	bridge
giant	bridge	page	change	edge	age	large	judge
page	giant	change	edge	judge	bridge	age	large
judge	large	bridge	age	edge	giant	page	change

Here are the words you copied in the last activity. Each row has the same words but in a different order. Please read all of the words as well as you can.

Your child reads the words going across each row. You may wish to place a card under the line she is reading to help her keep her place.

Correct any errors immediately.

Reading Two-Syllable Words

Have your child turn to page 18 of her workbook.

1.	respect	4.	power
2.	question	5.	private
3.	success	6.	object

Here is a list of words with two beats or syllables. For each word please underline

each syllable and say it. Then say the whole word.

Your child follows these steps for the remaining words:

1. She underlines the first syllable and says it.
2. She underlines the second syllable and says it.
3. She says the whole word.

NOTE: Keep in mind that the point of this exercise is to train students to look at every letter in a multisyllable word in a systematic way. The goal is NOT to teach syllablication rules. For this reason, there will often be more than one acceptable way to identify the syllables. The only requirements are that what your child underlines must be exactly one syllable and easy to say.

Notes about words

The *tion* in *question* is not pronounced /shun/ as it is in most words, but /chun/. This is because it is preceded by a /s/ sound, and in English, we don't have a /sh/ sound after /s/. Other words with this pattern include *combustion, congestion, digestion, exhaustion,* and *suggestion.* There is no need for you to say anything about this unless your child has difficulty reading the word. In that case, just underline the *tion* and say, "*In this word, this is /chun/.*"

Additional practice

Have your child continue to practice these words in subsequent lessons until she can read them easily. It is fine for her to read the whole word for practice without reading the parts. However, if she has difficulties with a word, she should read it one syllable at a time before saying the whole word.

If your child is good at reading the individual syllables but has problems blending the syllables into whole words, you should do an oral blending warm-up before a practice session. To conduct the oral blending practice, say the syllables one at a time with a 1 second pause in between and have your child say the whole word. This should be an exclusively oral activity. That is, do not have your child look at the written words when doing this, but just respond to the syllables you say.

Completing Sentences

Have your child turn to page 19 of her workbook.

Here is another page with sentences that have missing words. Your job is to fill in the choice that makes the most sense.

Remember to say blank when you come to the blank line.

Your child should read the first sentence, saying *blank* when she comes to the blank line.

She should select the word under the blank that makes the most sense and copy it on the blank line.

Have your child proceed in this way with the remaining sentences. The sentences continue on page 20.

NOTE: If your child has great difficulty with handwriting, it's fine for you yourself to write the words on the blank lines. If you do so, however, make sure that your child dictates the sounds of the word to you one at a time.

The correctly completed sentences are below.

1. Don't step too close to the <u>edge</u> of the street.

2. Please turn to <u>page</u> sixty-one.

3. I would like a <u>large</u> cup of coffee.

4. The <u>giant</u> chased Jack down the beanstalk.

5. The <u>judge</u> said, "Order in the court!"

6. My little sister never acts her <u>age</u>.

7. We drove over the <u>bridge</u>.

8. Someone needs to <u>change</u> the baby's diaper.

9. There was a <u>large</u> crowd at the ball game.

10. I have to do one more <u>page</u> in my workbook.

Unit Checkouts

Before moving on to the next unit, your child should be able to do the following accurately and without much hesitation:

1. Read the 8 target words in the unit easily.

2. Read the two-syllable words in the unit easily.

3. Read the sentences presented in the *Completing Sentences* fluently with virtually 100% accuracy.

e ea ai ie a ay

3

Unit Three

Lesson 5

In this lesson your child will:

- sort ways to spell the /e/ sound
- play *I Spy*
- analyze 8 target words with the /e/ sound

Sorting Words with e ea ai ie a ay

Have your child open her workbook to pages 22 and 23.

Today you will be reading words that have the /e/ sound.

NOTE: You are saying a SOUND, not a letter name.

Please say /e/.

Your child says the sound.

Point to the column headings on page 23.

There are 6 different ways to spell this sound. You're going to sort how it is spelled.

1 e	2 ea	3 ai	4 ie	5 a	6 ay

Please read the first word.

Point to the word *went* on page 22 and have your child read it.

NOTE: It's fine if the student recognizes the whole word and calls it out without saying the individual sounds first.

Nice job. Now find which column we should put this word in. Where do you see the match for how /e/ is spelled?

Your child should indicate that the word goes in column 1.

That's right. Please say-and-write <u>went</u> in column 1.

Your child should say the sounds in the word one at a time. Each time she says a sound, she should write how it is spelled.

Repeat these steps for the remaining words:

1. Your child reads the word.

2. She indicates in which column the word goes.

3. She records the word in the appropriate column on her sorting sheet. When she records the word, she should say each sound in the word in isolation as she writes how that sound is spelled.

The figure below shows what the completed sorting sheet should look like.

1 e	2 ea	3 ai	4 ie	5 a	6 ay
went	bread	said	friend	many	says
letter	head				
tell	breath				
kept					
spell					

VARIATIONS: Instead of having your child write the words on a sorting sheet, you may wish to write the sorting words on separate note cards and have your child sort the cards. If you do so, make sure to write the words with the spacing used on page 22 of the student workbook. You should also write the column headings *e, ea, ai*, etc. on separate cards to help your child sort. This variation allows you to reduce the amount that your child has to write. You may also choose to use the sorting sheet but record each word yourself after your child has read it and indicated in which column it should go.

Breaking Words Apart

Have your child turn to page 24 of her workbook.

Here is another list of words to practice. Please read the first word and then copy it in your workbook.

Your child reads the word and copies it.

You should write the word also on a dry erase board so that you can model the markings she is about to do.

Nice work. Now say each sound in the word and underline how it is spelled.

Repeat these steps for the remaining words:

1. Your child reads the word.

2. She copies the word neatly in her workbook.

3. She says the sounds of the word one at a time. As she says a sound, she underlines how that sound is spelled.

If your child is ever confused about how a particular sound is spelled, tell your child very directly.

NOTE: The word <u>ready</u> has two syllables. When your child records this word, she should say the word in syllables and write each syllable on a separate line. Also, you should allow any syllable division so long as each part is exactly one syllable and easy to say. In other words, either read-y or rea-dy is acceptable.

The following figure shows the correct markings for the words.

1. b r ea th		5. t a ke	
2. b r ea d		6. t a ck	
3. h ea d		7. l a ke	
4. r ea d y		8. l a ck	

I Spy

Have your child turn to page 25 of her workbook.

Now you get to play a game of I Spy. Underline ge, dge, or ce.

Your child goes through the list underlining any words with the three target graphemes.

Please read all of the words.

Have your child read the words. Repeat as necessary until she can read all of the words accurately without much hesitation.

The following figure shows the correct markings for the words.

1. for<u>ce</u>		6. stran<u>ge</u>	
2. oran<u>ge</u>		7. ple<u>dge</u>	
3. e<u>dge</u>		8. pea<u>ce</u>	
4. smu<u>dge</u>		9. voi<u>ce</u>	
5. poun<u>ce</u>		10. fen<u>ce</u>	

Lesson 6

In this lesson your child will:
- practice reading the target words for the unit
- read some two-syllable words
- complete some sentences with the target words for the unit

Word Reading Practice

Have your child turn to page 26 of her workbook.

head	lack	ready	bread	breath	take	tack	lake
lack	lake	bread	tack	head	breath	take	ready
bread	breath	take	head	ready	lake	lack	tack
ready	take	tack	breath	lack	head	lake	bread

Here are the words you copied in the last activity. Each row has the same words but in a different order. Please read all of the words as well as you can.

Your child reads the words going across each row. You may wish to place a card under the line she is reading to help her keep her place.

Correct any errors immediately.

Reading Two-Syllable Words

Have your child turn to page 27 of her workbook.

1. direct		4. final	
2. wooden		5. decide	
3. person		6. wonder	

Here is a list of words with two beats or syllables. For each word please underline each syllable and say it. Then say the whole word.

Your child follows these steps for the remaining words:
1. She underlines the first syllable and says it.
2. She underlines the second syllable and says it.
3. She says the whole word.

NOTE: Keep in mind that the point of this exercise is to train students to look at every letter in a multisyllable word in a systematic way. The goal is NOT to teach syllablication rules. For this reason, there will often be more than one acceptable way to identify the syllables. The only requirements are that what your child underlines must be exactly one syllable and easy to say.

Additional practice

Have your child continue to practice these words in subsequent lessons until she can read them easily. It is fine for her to read the whole word for practice without reading the parts. However, if she has difficulties with a word, she should read it one syllable at a time before saying the whole word.

If your child is good at reading the individual syllables but has problems blending the syllables into whole words, you should do an oral blending warm-up before a practice session. To conduct the oral blending practice, say the syllables one at a time with a 1 second pause in between and have your child say the whole word. This should be an exclusively oral activity. That is, do not have your child look at the written words when doing this, but just respond to the syllables you say.

<u>Completing Sentences</u>

Have your child turn to page 28 of her workbook.

Here is another page with sentences that have missing words. Your job is to fill in the choice that makes the most sense.

Remember to say <u>blank</u> when you come to the blank line.

Your child should read the first sentence, saying <u>blank</u> when she comes to the blank line.

She should select the word underneath the blank line that yields a sensible sentence and copy it on the blank line.

Have your child proceed in this way with the remaining sentences. The sentences continue on page 29.

NOTE: If your child has great difficulty with hand-writing, it's fine for you yourself to write the words on the blank lines. If you do so, however, make sure that your child dictates the sounds of the word to you one at a time as you write it.

The completed sheets should look like the following figure.

1.	I'm <u>ready</u> to start my work now..
2.	We bought some good <u>bread</u> at the bakery.
3.	Tom needs thumb <u>tacks</u> to put up his poster.
4.	Let's <u>take</u> the dog with us to the park.
5.	Our coach said we had a <u>lack</u> of effort.
6.	Have you ever been to the Finger <u>Lakes</u>?
7.	Jill got to be at the <u>head</u> of the line.
8.	After the race I was out of <u>breath</u>.
9.	We will get <u>ready</u> for dinner right away.
10.	I can hold my <u>breath</u> for about 30 seconds

<u>Unit Checkouts</u>

Before moving on to the next unit, your child should be able to do the following accurately and without much hesitation:

1. Read the 8 target words in the unit easily.

2. Read the two-syllable words in the unit easily.

3. Read the sentences presented in the *Completing Sentences* fluently with virtually 100% accuracy.

o a

Unit Four
4

Lesson 7

In this lesson your child will:

• sort ways to spell the /o/ sound

• analyze 8 target words with the /o/ sound

Sorting Words with o and a

Have your child open her workbook to pages 32 and 33.

Today you will be reading words that have the /o/ sound.

NOTE: You are saying a SOUND, not letter names.

Please say /o/.

Your child repeats the sound.

Point to the column headings on page 33.

There are 2 different ways to spell this sound. You're going to sort how the /o/ sound is spelled.

1 o	2 a	

Please read the first word.

Point to the word *swap* on page 32.

NOTE: It's fine if your child recognizes the whole word and calls it out without saying the individual sounds first.

Nice job. Now find which column we should put this word in. Where do you see the match for how /o/ is spelled?

Your child should indicate that the word goes in column 2.

That's right. Please say-and-write _swap_ in column 2.

Your child should say the sounds in the word one at a time. Each time she says a sound she should write how it is spelled.

Repeat these steps for the remaining words:

1. Your child reads the word.

2. She indicates in which column the word goes.

3. She records the word in the appropriate column on her sorting sheet. When she records the word, she should say each sound in the word in isolation as she writes how that sound is spelled.

Notes on words

The letter *a* following a *w* typically represents the /o/ sound, as exemplified by the words in this sort. The letter *a* after *qu* also frequently represents /o/, as in *quality* and *quantity*, but these *qua* words are at a reading level above that covered in this workbook.

The figure below shows what the completed sorting sheet should look like.

1 o	2 a	
lock	swap	swan
stop	watch	
not	wasp	
frost	waffle	
rock	swamp	
	wand	

VARIATIONS: Instead of having your child write the words on the sorting sheet, you may wish to write the sorting words on separate note cards and have your child sort the cards. If you do so, make sure to write the words with the spacing in the list on page 32 of the student workbook. You should also write the column headings *o* and *a* on separate cards to help your child sort. This variation allows you to reduce the amount that your child has to write. You may also choose to use the sorting sheet but record each word yourself after your child has read it and indicated in which column it should go.

Breaking Words Apart

Have your child turn to page 34 of her workbook.

Here is another list of words to practice. Please read the first word and then copy it in your notebook.

Your child reads the word and copies it.

Nice work. Now say each sound in the word and underline how it is spelled.

Repeat these steps for the remaining words:

1. Your child reads the word.

2. She copies the word neatly in her workbook.

3. She says the sounds of the word one at a time. As she says a sound, she underlines how that sound is spelled.

If your child is ever confused about how a particular sound is spelled, tell her very directly.

NOTE: The word <u>swallow</u> has two syllables. When your child records this word, she should say the word in syllables and write each syllable on a separate line.

The following figure shows the correct markings for the words.

1.	<u>s w a</u> <u>ll ow</u>	5.	<u>b a ck</u>
2.	<u>w a sh</u>	6.	<u>b a k e</u>
3.	<u>w a n t</u>	7.	<u>s n a ck</u>
4.	<u>w a tch</u>	8.	<u>s n a k e</u>

Lesson 8

In this lesson your child will:

- practice reading the target words for the unit
- read some two-syllable words
- complete some sentences with the target words for the unit

Word Reading Practice

Have your child turn to page 35 of her workbook.

want	snake	watch	wash	swallow	back	bake	snake
wash	swallow	back	want	watch	snack	snake	bake
watch	back	bake	swallow	snake	want	snack	wash
back	bake	snake	snack	wash	watch	water	want

Here are the words you copied in the last activity. Each row has the same words but in a different order. Please read all of the words as well as you can.

Your child reads the words going across each row. You may wish to place a card under the line she is reading to help her keep her place.

Correct any errors immediately.

Reading Two-Syllable Words

Have your child turn to page 36 of her workbook.

1.	common	4.	figure
2.	pattern	5.	slightly
3.	battle	6.	council

Here is a list of words with two beats or syllables. For each word please underline each syllable and say it. Then say the whole word.

Your child follows these steps for the remaining words:

1. She underlines the first syllable and says it.
2. She underlines the second syllable and says it.
3. She says the whole word.

NOTE: Keep in mind that the point of this exercise is to train students to look at every letter in a multisyllable word in a systematic way. The goal is NOT to teach syllablication rules. For this reason, there will often be more than one acceptable way to identify the syllables. The only requirements are that what your child underlines must be exactly one syllable and easy to say.

Additional practice

Have your child continue to practice these words in subsequent lessons until she can read them easily. It is fine for her to read the whole word for practice without reading the parts. However, if she has difficulties with a word, she should read it one syllable at a time before saying the whole word.

If your child is good at reading the individual syllables but has problems blending the syllables into whole words, you should do an oral blending warm-up before a practice session. To conduct the oral blending practice, say the syllables one at a time with a 1 second pause in between and have your child say the whole word. This should be an exclusively oral activity. That is, do not have your child look at the written words when doing this, but just respond to the syllables you say.

Completing Sentences

Have your child turn to page 37 of her workbook.

Here is another page with sentences that have missing words. Your job is to fill in the choice that makes the most sense.

Remember to say <u>blank</u> when you come to the blank line.

Your child should read the first sentence, saying <u>blank</u> when she comes to the blank line.

She should select the word underneath the blank that makes the most sense and write it on the line.

Have your child proceed in this way with the remaining sentences. The sentences continue on page 38.

NOTE: If your child has great difficulty with handwriting, it's fine for you yourself to write the words on the blank lines. If you do so, however, make sure that your child dictates the sounds of the word to you one at a time as you write it.

The completed sheet should look like the following figure.

1. You should <u>wash</u> that shirt in cold water.

2. Tom wanted to <u>watch</u> the game on TV.

3. What do you <u>want</u> to have for dinner.

4. The <u>back</u> door of the school is locked.

5. We found a garden <u>snake</u> in our backyard.

6. My favorite <u>snack</u> is milk and cookies.

7. Sam knows how to <u>bake</u> brownies.

8. Do you <u>want</u> to play on the swings?

9. I want to <u>watch</u> your team play football.

10. Did you <u>swallow</u> all that milk in one gulp.

Unit Checkouts

Before moving on to the next unit, your child should be able to do the following accurately and without much hesitation:

1. Read the 8 target words in the unit easily.

2. Read the two-syllable words in the unit easily.

3. Read the sentences presented in the *Completing Sentences* activity fluently and with virtually 100% accuracy.

u-e u ue ew you

5

Unit Five

Lesson 9

In this lesson your child will:

• sort ways to spell the /ue/ sound

• analyze 8 target words with the /ue/ sound

• play *I Spy*

Sorting Words with u-e u ue ew you

Have your child open her workbook to pages 40 and 41.

Today you will be reading words that have the sound /ue/.

NOTE: You are saying a SOUND, not a letter name.

Please say /ue/.

Your child repeats the sound.

Point to the headings on page 41 of her workbook.

There are 5 different ways to spell this sound. You're going to sort how the /ue/ sound is spelled.

1 u-e	2 u	3 ue	4 ew	5 you

Repeat these steps for each word:

1. Your child reads the word.

2. She indicates in which column the word goes.

3. She records the word in the appropriate column on her sorting sheet. When she records the word, she should say each sound in the word in isolation as she writes how that sound is spelled.

The figure below shows what the completed sorting sheet should look like.

1 u-e	2 u	3 ue	4 ew	5 you
cube	pupil	argue	few	you
mule	human	rescue		
huge	music			
mute				
cute				

VARIATIONS: Instead of having your child write the words on a sorting sheet, you may wish to write the sorting words on separate note cards and have your child sort the cards. If you do so, make sure to write the words with the spacing in the list of words on the facing page. You should also write the column headings *u-e, ue, ew,* and *you* on separate cards to help your child sort. This variation allows you to reduce the amount that your child has to write. You may also choose to use the sorting sheet but record each word yourself after your child has read it and indicated in which column it should go.

Notes about words

In Level B1 students sorted ways to spell the /ew/ sound as in the words *food* and *new*. The sound students sort in this present activity, often referred to in some reading programs as the "long-u" sound, is related but different. This sound is technically two sounds, the /y/ sound in front of the /ew/ sound. However, the English spelling system often uses a single grapheme to spell this sound. Although this may seem complicated, for native English speakers, words with this sound do not typically pose any real decoding difficulties because readers will readily flex the vowel sound to come up with the proper word. For instance, if a person first decoded the word *human* as /hewman/ (to rhyme with *Truman*), he would, especially when reading the word in context, readily change the vowel sound to /ue/ in order to render a meaningful word.

Breaking Words Apart

Have your child turn to page 42 of her workbook.

Here is another list of words to practice. Please read the first word and then copy it in your workbook.

Your child reads the word and copies it.

Nice work. Now say each sound in the word and underline how it is spelled.

Repeat these steps for the remaining words:

1. Your child reads the word.

2. She copies the word neatly in her workbook.

3. She says the sounds of the word one at a time. As she says a sound, she underlines how that sound is spelled.

If your child is ever confused about how a particular sound is spelled, tell your child very directly.

NOTE: The words ever, even, and every each have more than one syllable. When your child records these words, she should say the word in syllables and write each syllable on a separate line.

The following figure shows the correct markings for the words.

1. u s e	5. h u g e
2. u s ed	6. e v er
3. c u t e	7. e v e n
4. f ew	8. e v er y

I Spy

Have your child turn to page 43 of her workbook.

Please write the 3 patterns where the letter c is /s/.

Your child writes *ce, ci, cy*. If your child says she doesn't remember any of the patterns, write *ce* and see if that triggers her to remember the other 2 patterns. If not, write all three patterns, have your child copy and recite them out loud, and then review intermittently throughout the lesson.

Now please underline all the words on this list that fit the pattern.

Your child underlines the appropriate words.

Now please read all of the words. Remember, if the word fits the pattern, you'll say /s/.

Have your child read the words. Repeat as necessary until she can read all of the words accurately without much hesitation.

The following figure shows the correct markings for the words.

1. place	6. picnic
2. music	7. city
3. clean	8. copy
4. dance	9. Nancy
5. cloth	10. public

Lesson 10

In this lesson your child will:

• practice reading the target words for the unit

• read some two-syllable words

• complete some sentences with the target words for the unit

Word Reading Practice

Have your child turn to page 44 of her workbook.

every	even	used	ever	cute	use	huge	few
used	use	huge	cute	few	even	every	ever
few	huge	ever	use	every	cute	even	used
huge	ever	every	even	used	few	use	cute

Here are the words you copied in the last activity. Each row has the same words but in a different order. Please read all of the words as well as you can.

Your child reads the words going across each row. You may wish to place a card under the line she is reading to help her keep her place.

Correct any errors immediately.

Reading Two-Syllable Words

Have your child turn to page 45 of her workbook.

	tion	ture
1. action	4. section	
2. capture	5. nature	
3. station	6. picture	

In this activity you will introduce your child to the endings *tion* and *ture*.

We're going to look at two-syllable words that end with some spellings we haven't discussed yet. Here is the first new spelling.

Point to *tion* at the top of the page.

When you see this at the end of a word, you should say /shun/. We're not going to break this syllable down into individual sounds, but you will learn it as a whole. When I point to it, say /shun/.

Point to the syllable *tion* several times. Each time you point, your child should say /shun/. Repeat 3 or 4 times, or as long as necessary to get a firm response.

Here's the other new ending.

Point to *ture* at the top of the page.

This is /cher/. When I point to it, say /cher/.

Point to the syllable *ture* several times. Each time you point, your child should say /cher/. Repeat 3 or 4 times, or as long as necessary to get a firm response.

Great job! Now let's practice writing these. The best way to learn them is to say the letter names out loud. /Shun/ is spelled tee-i-oh-en. Now it's your turn. Say the letter names as I point to them.

Point to each letter in turn and have your child say the letter name. Repeat several times. The last few times you should stop pointing at the letters and just have your child say the letter names.

Repeat these steps to have your child spell *ture*.

Great job! Now I'm going to cover up this page and you have to write the two new special endings. As you write them, please say the letter names quietly to yourself.

Dictate /shun/ and /cher/ to your child. After she has written the syllable, uncover the page and have her check her own work. If she made a mistake, have her repeat the spelling of the syllable out loud several times and then cover up the page again and have her write the syllable. Review intermittently throughout the remainder of the lesson.

Here is another list of words with two beats or syllables. All of these words end in either /shun/ or /cher/. For each word please underline each syllable and say it. Then say the whole word.

Your child follows these steps for the remaining words:

1. She underlines the first syllable and says it.

2. She underlines the second syllable and says it.

3. She says the whole word.

NOTE: Keep in mind that the point of this exercise is to train students to look at every letter in a multisyllable word in a systematic way. The goal is NOT to teach syllablication rules. For this reason, there will often be more than one acceptable way to identify the syllables. The only require-

ments are that what your child underlines must be exactly one syllable and easy to say.

Additional practice

Have your child continue to practice these words in subsequent lessons until she can read them easily. It is fine for her to read the whole word for practice without reading the parts. However, if she has difficulties with a word, she should read it one syllable at a time before saying the whole word.

If your child is good at reading the individual syllables but has problems blending the syllables into whole words, you should do an oral blending warm-up before a practice session. To conduct the oral blending practice, say the syllables one at a time with a 1 second pause in between and have your child say the whole word. This should be an exclusively oral activity. That is, do not have your child look at the written words when doing this, but just respond to the syllables you say.

Completing Sentences

Have your child turn to page 46 of her workbook.

Here is another page with sentences that have missing words. Your job is to fill in the choice that makes the most sense.

Remember to say <u>blank</u> when you come to the blank line.

Your child should read the first sentence, saying *blank* when she comes to the blank line.

Your child should select the word underneath the blan that makes the most sense and copy it on the line.

Have your child proceed in this way with the remaining sentences.

NOTE: If your child has great difficulty with handwriting, it's fine for you yourself to write the words on the blank lines. If you do so, however, make sure that your child dictates the sounds of the word to you one at a time as you write it.

The completed sentences should look like the following figure.

1.	Have you ever seen this <u>cute</u> picture of me?
2.	I would like to <u>use</u> your baseball glove.
3.	Sam got a <u>huge</u> candy bar at the store.
4.	Tom didn't <u>even</u> try to catch the ball.
5.	I got you something at the <u>used</u> book store.
6.	We should be leaving in a <u>few</u> minutes.
7.	Have you <u>ever</u> eaten a better cake?
8.	We ate <u>every</u> single piece of it.
9.	The school play was a <u>huge</u> success.
10.	Jill used <u>every</u> one of our paint brushes.

Unit Checkouts

Before moving on to the next unit, your child should be able to do the following accurately and without much hesitation:

1. Read the 8 target words in the unit easily.

2. Read the two-syllable words in the unit easily.

3. Read the sentences presented in the Completing Sentences activity easily.

i y e

6

Unit Six

Lesson 11

In this lesson your child will:

- sort ways to spell the /i/ sound
- read words that end in *ies*
- read sentences with *ies* words
- analyze 8 target words with the /i/ sound

Sorting Words with i y e

Have your child open her workbook to pages 50 and 51.

Today you will be reading words that have the sound /i/.

NOTE: You are saying a SOUND, not a letter name.

Please say /i/.

Your child repeats the sound.

Point to the column headings on page 51.

There are 3 different ways to spell this sound. You're going to sort how the /i/ sound is spelled.

1 i	2 y	3 e

Repeat these steps for each word:

1. Your child reads the word.

2. She indicates in which column the word goes.

3. She records the word in the appropriate column on her sorting sheet. When she records the word, she should say each sound in the word in isolation as she writes how that sound is spelled.

The figure below shows what the completed sorting sheet should look like.

1 i	2 y	3 e
filled	gym	pretty
inch	Egypt	
kids	myth	
pick	system	
rich	gypsy	
skin		

VARIATIONS: Instead of having your child write the words on a sorting sheet, you may wish to write the sorting words on separate note cards and have your child sort the cards. If you do so, make sure to write the words with the spacing in the list at the top of the page. You should also write the column headings *i, y, e* on separate cards to help your child sort. This variation allows you to reduce the amount that your child has to write. You may also choose to use the sorting sheet but record each word yourself after your child has read it and indicated in which column it should go.

Notes about words

We frequently see the letter *y* at the beginning of a syllable representing a consonant sound (*yes*), at the end of a word representing an /ee/ or /ie/ sound (*happy, try*), and as part of a vowel digraph (*day, key, toy*), but much more rarely as a vowel in the middle of a syllable (as in the words in column 2 of this sort). Because a medial *y* appears relatively infrequently, readers often become confused about how to decode it. A simple and effective technique is to tell the student that the *y* represents the same sounds as the (much more commonly used) letter *i*, and have her write a little *i* above the *y* on the word and sound it out using the same sounds one would use for i. This usually makes words with *y* much easier to decode.

i
system

Reading Words with "ies"

Many students are confused when they come across a word such as *carries* that ends in *ies*. The key to decoding words with this ending involves recognizing that the underlying base word ends in *y* and has been transformed into a plural (if it's a noun) or third person singular (if it's a verb).

The purpose of this exercise is to help students recognize that these *ies* words come from base words that end in *y*.

Have your child turn to page 52 of her workbook.

carry	carries
baby	babies
party	parties
fly	flies
cry	cries

When we add <u>s</u> to a word that ends in <u>y</u>, like carry. . .

Point to the word *carry*.

. . .we make a couple of spelling changes. First the letter <u>y</u> changes to <u>i</u>.

Underline the *i* in *carries*.

In addition we don't add plain old <u>s</u> but <u>es</u>."

Underline the *es* in *carries*.

So this is the word <u>carry</u>, and when I add s it becomes <u>carries</u>.

Point to the appropriate words on the page as you say them.

Now it's your turn to read these words.

Have your child read the words going across, beginning with the words *carry* and *carries*.

If your child has difficulty reading any of the *ies* words, help him by having him complete the appropriate sentence below.

1. We don't say, "He carry the bags," but "He . . ."

2. We don't say, "All of the baby are hungry," but "All of the . . ."

3. We don't say, "I went to many birthday party," but "I went to many birthday . . ."

4. We don't say, "She fly in an airplane," but "She . . ."

5. We don't say, "The young child cry," but, "The young child . . ."

If your child still can't read the *ies* word correctly after you give the above prompt, tell her the word and have her repeat. Then review the words intermittently throughout the remainder of the lesson.

Sentence Reading Practice

Have your child turn to page 53 of her workbook.

Here are some sentences with the words you just read. Please read these sentences as well as you can.

Your child reads the sentences. Correct any errors immediately, but give her plenty of time to figure out the two syllable words.

Have your child re-read this page throughout the day as necessary until she can read it easily.

1.	The baby cries when he is hungry.
2.	Tom will go to three birthday parties this week.
3.	Sam carries a very large backpack.
4.	Time flies when you're having fun.
5.	All of the babies were sleeping.

Breaking Words Apart

Have your child turn to page 54 of her workbook. Follow these steps for each word:

1. Your child reads the word.

2. She copies the word neatly in her workbook.

3. She says the sounds of the word one at a time. As she says a sound, she underlines how that sound is spelled.

If your child is ever confused about how a particular sound is spelled, tell your child very directly.

The following figure shows the correct markings for the words.

1. <u>g</u> <u>y</u> <u>m</u>	5. <u>f</u> <u>r</u> <u>o</u> <u>m</u>
2. <u>m</u> <u>y</u> <u>th</u>	6. <u>f</u> <u>or</u>
3. <u>p</u> <u>re</u> <u>tt</u> <u>y</u>	7. <u>c</u> <u>o</u> <u>m</u> <u>e</u>
4. <u>of</u>	8. <u>c</u> <u>a</u> <u>m</u> <u>e</u>

Notes about words:

Pretty: Have your child say /e/ when underlining the *e*, but pronounce the blended word as it is normally pronounced. Also, this word is two-syllables. When your child says it, she should say it in two syllables and write each syllable on a separate line before underlining how each sound is spelled.

Of: Don't have your child sound out the individual sounds. Rather, have her underline the whole word and say /uv/. The word is presented here because many children confuse it with the word *from*. Both have been provided so that students will have the opportunity to pay attention closely to the contrast in spellings between the two words.

Lesson 12

In this lesson your child will:

- practice reading the target words for the unit
- read some two-syllable words
- complete some sentences with the target words for the unit

Word Reading Practice

Have your child turn to page 55 of her workbook.

came	come	myth	for	pretty	gym	from	of
myth	gym	from	pretty	of	come	came	for
of	from	for	gym	came	pretty	come	myth
from	for	came	come	myth	of	gym	pretty

Here are the words you copied in the last activity. Each row has the same words but in a different order. Please read all of the words as well as you can.

Your child reads the words going across each row. You may wish to place a card under the line she is reading to help her keep her place.

Correct any errors immediately.

Reading Two-Syllable Words

Have your child turn to page 56 of her workbook.

ac<u>tion</u> na<u>ture</u>	
1. against	4. creature
2. fraction	5. carries
3. season	6. motion

Point to *action* and *nature* at the top of the page.

Here are two key words to help you remember how to read the special endings /shun/ and /ture/. Please read these words.

Have your child read the words. If she has difficulty, tell her how to pronounce the underlined part (that is, either *tion* or *ture*) and then have her sound out the words. Review these words intermittently throughout the lesson.

Now tell me the sound for just the underlined part.

Your child says /shun/ when looking at *action* and /cher/ when looking at *nature*. Repeat as necessary until your child can say these syllables accurately and quickly when looking at the key word.

Here is another list of words with two beats or syllables. Some of the words have /shun/ or /cher/, but not all of them.

For each word please underline each syllable and say it. Then say the whole word.

Your child follows these steps for the remaining words:

1. She underlines the first syllable and says it.
2. She underlines the second syllable and says it.
3. She says the whole word.

NOTE: Keep in mind that the point of this exercise is to train students to look at every letter in a multisyllable word in a systematic way. The goal is NOT to teach syllablication rules. For this reason, there will often be more than one acceptable way to identify the syllables. The only requirements are that what your child underlines must be exactly one syllable and easy to say.

Additional practice

Have your child continue to practice these words in subsequent lessons until she can read them easily. It is fine for her to read the whole word for practice without reading the parts. However, if she has difficulties with a word, she should read it one syllable at a time before saying the whole word.

If your child is good at reading the individual syllables but has problems blending the syllables into whole words, you should do an oral blending warm-up before a practice session. To conduct the oral blending practice, say the syllables one at a time with a 1 second pause in between and have your child say the whole word. This should be an exclusively oral activity. That is, do not have your child look at the written words when doing this, but just respond to the syllables you say.

Completing Sentences

Have your child turn to page 57 of her workbook.

Here is the page with some sentences for you to complete. Fill in the blank with the word from the two choices that makes the most sense.

Remember to say <u>blank</u> when you come to the blank line.

Your child should read the first sentence, saying <u>blank</u> when she comes to the blank line.

Your child should select the word underneath the blank that makes the most sense and write it on the line.

Have your child proceed in this way with the remaining sentences. The sentences continue on page 58.

NOTE: If your child has great difficulty with handwriting, it's fine for you yourself to write the words on the blank lines. If you do so, however, make sure that your child dictates the sounds of the word to you one at a time as you write it.

The following figure shows the sentences completed correctly.

1. We had a good time in <u>gym</u> class today.

2. Tom is studying Greek <u>myths</u> in school.

3. I hope that the test is <u>pretty</u> easy.

4. Jill has <u>come</u> a long way to see us.

5. That cheese comes <u>from</u> Switzerland.

6. All <u>of</u> my friends can come to my party.

7. I haven't seen Sam <u>for</u> a few weeks.

8. These presents are <u>from</u> Mom and Dad.

9. I read a <u>myth</u> about how humans got fire.

10. Tom drew a <u>pretty</u> picture of his sister.

Unit Checkouts

Before moving on to the next unit, your child should be able to do the following accurately and without much hesitation:

1. Read the 8 target words in the unit easily.

2. Read the two-syllable words in the unit easily.

3. Read the sentences presented in the *Completing Sentences* activity easily.

a

7
Unit Seven

Lesson 13

In this lesson your child will:

- sort a list of two-syllable words with the letter *a* in the first syllable depending upon what sound that letter represents
- flex nonsense words with *a*
- analyze 8 target words

Sorting Words with a

Up until this unit the introductory sorting exercise involved sorting the different ways a single sound was spelled. In this unit and all the remaining units of B2, the task changes to sorting a particular grapheme by the sound it represents. Units 7-11 will focus on flexing *a, e, i, o,* and *u* in two-syllable words. The remaining units will focus on the variation in sounds represented by the graphemes *ea, ou, ar,* and *ough.*

To begin the lesson, write the letter *a* on a dry erase board or a piece of paper.

Please tell me the two common sounds for this letter.

Elicit from your child the sounds /a/ and /ay/. If she doesn't know the sounds, write *at* and *lady* on the board, underlining the *a* in each, and ask her for the sounds of the underlined letter in each word.

Have your child open her workbook to pages 60-61.

NOTE: The words in the previous sorting tasks in Level B1 and B2 had all been presented with the graphemes separated by a space. Thus, for instance, the word "boat" was presented as b oa t. Beginning with this unit, all of the words on the sorting list will be presented without this special formatting.

Good job! This page has a list of two-syllable words with this letter. We're going to sort them according to whether you hear /a/ or /ay/ in the first syllable of each word. Please read the first word.

Your child reads the word. If she has difficulty reading the word, have her underline each syllable in turn and say it in isolation. You can also underline the *le* at the end of the word and say, "*This is /l/.*"

If your child pronounces the word with the /a/ sound, so that the word rhymes with *Scrabble,* say, "*There is no word /tabl/. You said an /a/ sound here (pointing to the a). What other sound can this be?*" Then have her sound out the word with the /ay/ sound.

What sound do you hear in the first syllable of table? /a/ or /ay/?

Your child should say /ay/. If she says /a/, tell her, "*That would make the word tabble*" (pronounce the word to rhyme with *Scrabble*) and then tell her the correct sound.

Let's put all the words with the /ay/ sound in column 1.

Have your child say-and-write *table* in column 1. Repeat these steps for the remaining words:

1. Have your child read the word. If she needs to, she can underline each syllable and say it in isolation.

2. Ask, "*What sound do you hear in the first syllable of <word>? /a/ or /ay/?*"

3. Help your child identify the correct sound.

4. Have your child say-and-write words with /ay/ in column 1 and words with /a/ in column 2.

The following figure shows what the completed sorting sheet should look like.

1	2
table	camel
maple	carry
nature	planet
crazy	Spanish
major	travel
danger	battle

Flexing Practice with "a"

In this exercise your child will practice flexing nonsense words with *a*. That is, she will read them first with the /a/ sound and then with the /ay/ sound.

Have your child turn to page 62 of the her workbook.

Here are some nonsense words we will use to practice flexing.

Read each word two ways, first with the /a/ sound and then with the /ay/ sound. I'll do the first three. Listen: ma may; pa pay; va vay.

Run your finger under the word each time you pronounce it.

Now it's your turn to read these 3 words. Your child reads the first three words. Make sure that she first reads each word with the /a/ sound.

After your child reads these words, she should continue flexing the remaining words.

If the task is difficult for her, review one column of words intermittently throughout the day.

Breaking Words Apart

Have your child turn to page 63 of her workbook.

Follow these steps for each word:

1. Your child reads the word.

2. She copies the word neatly in her workbook.

3. She says the sounds of the word one at a time. As she says a sound, she underlines how that sound is spelled.

If your child is ever confused about how a particular sound is spelled, tell her very directly.

NOTE: Each of the first four words on the list have two-syllables. When your child records these words, she should say the words in syllables and record each syllable on a separate line.

The following figure shows the correct markings for the words.

1.	t͟a b͟le	5.	l͟i͟ck
2.	c͟r͟a z͟y	6.	l͟i͟k͟e
3.	b͟a tt͟le	7.	n͟o͟t
4.	t͟r͟a v͟el	8.	n͟o͟t͟e

Lesson 14

In this lesson your child will:

- practice reading the target words for the unit
- complete some sentences with the target words for the unit

Word Reading Practice

Have your child turn to page 64 of her workbook.

note	not	crazy	lick	battle	table	like	travel
crazy	table	like	battle	travel	not	note	lick
travel	like	lick	table	note	battle	not	crazy
table	crazy	like	note	lick	battle	not	travel

Here are the words you copied in the last activity. Each row has the same words but in a different order. Please read all of the words as well as you can.

Your child reads the words going across each row. You may wish to place a card under the line she is reading to help her keep her place.

Correct any errors immediately.

Completing Sentences

Have your child turn to page 65 of her workbook.

Here is the page with some sentences for you to complete. Fill in the blank with the word

from the two choices that makes the most sense.

Remember to say blank when you come to the blank line.

Your child should read the first sentence, saying blank when she comes to the blank line.

Your child should select the word underneath the blank line that makes the most sense and copy it on the blank line.

Have your child proceed in this way with the remaining sentences. The sentences continue on page 66.

NOTE: If your child has great difficulty with hand-writing, it's fine for you yourself to write the words on the blank lines. If you do so, however, make sure that your child dictates the sounds of the word to you one at a time as you write it.

The completed sheet should look like the following figure.

1.	I like to travel to a warm spot in the winter.
2.	The two teams fought a fierce battle.
3.	We thought that Tom's idea was crazy.
4.	We can play the game on our kitchen table.
5.	Did Dad like the book I gave him?
6.	Mom left a note for us on the table.
7.	Jill did not want to go shopping with us.
8.	My dog likes to lick my face.
9.	Soon our class will travel to Washington, D.C.
10.	Let's eat at that table over there.

Unit Checkouts

Before moving on to the next unit, your child should be able to do the following accurately and without much hesitation:

1. Read the 8 target words in the unit easily.

2. Read the sentences presented in the Completing Sentences activity easily.

e

Unit Eight
8

Lesson 15

In this lesson your child will:

- sort a list of two-syllable words with the letter *e* in the first syllable depending upon what sound that letter represents
- flex nonsense words with *e*
- analyze 8 target words

Sorting Words with e

Write the letter *e* on a dry erase board or a piece of paper.

Please tell me the two common sounds for this letter.

Elicit from your child the sounds /e/ and /ea/. If she doesn't know the sounds, writes *Ed* and *be* on the board, underlining the *e* in each, and asks her for the sounds of the underlined letter in each word.

Have your child open her workbook to pages 68-69.

Good job! This page has a list of two-syllable words with this letter. We're going to sort them according to whether you hear /e/ or /ee/ in the first syllable of each word.

Please read the first word.

Your child reads the word. If she has difficulty reading the word, have her underline each syllable in turn and say it in isolation.

What sound do you hear in the first syllable of secret? /e/ or /ee/?

Your child should say /ee/. If she says /e/, tell her, "*That would make the word /secret/*" (pronounce the word the same way you pronounce the first two syllables of *secretary*) and then tell her the correct sound.

Let's put all the words with the /ee/ sound in column 1.

Have your child say-and-write *secret* in column 1.

Repeat these steps for the remaining words:

1. Have your child read the word. If she needs to, she can underline each syllable and say it in isolation.

2. Ask, "*What sound do you hear in the first syllable of <word>? /e/ or /ee/?*"

3. Help your child identify the correct sound.

4. Have your child say-and-write words with /ee/ in column 1 and words with /e/ in column 2.

The following figure shows what the completed sorting sheet should look like.

1	2
secret	ever
begin	lemon
legal	melon
evil	metal
even	seven
rebate	second

Flexing Practice with "e"

In this exercise your child will practice flexing nonsense words with *e*. That is, she will read them first with the /e/ sound and then with the /ee/ sound.

Have your child turn to page 70 of the her workbook.

Here are some nonsense words we will use to practice flexing.

Read each word two ways, first with the /e/ sound and then with the /ee/ sound. I'll do the first three. Listen: me mee; pe pee; ve vee.

NOTE: When you say /me/, /pe/, and /ve/ above, you should pronounce them so that they sound like the first two sounds of met, pet, and vet, respectively.

Run your finger under the word each time you pronounce it.

Now it's your turn to read these 3 words. Your child reads the first three words. Make sure that she first reads each word with the /e/ sound.

After your child reads these words, she should continue flexing the remaining words.

If the task is difficult for her, review one column of words intermittently throughout the day.

Breaking Words Apart

Have your child turn to page 71 of her workbook.

Follow these steps for each word:

1. Your child reads the word.

2. She copies the word neatly in her workbook.

3. She says the sounds of the word one at a time. As she says a sound, she underlines how that sound is spelled.

If your child is ever confused about how a particular sound is spelled, tell her very directly.

NOTE: All of the words on the list except for spies and tries have two-syllables. When your child records the two-syllable words, she should say the words in syllables and write each syllable on a separate line.

The following figure shows the correct markings for the words.

1. s e c r e t		5. s p i e s	
2. s e c o n d		6. t r i e s	
3. e v er		7. h u rr i e s	
4. e v e n		8. p u pp i e s	

Lesson 16

In this lesson your child will:

• practice reading the target words for the unit

• complete some sentences with the target words for the unit

Word Reading Practice

Have your child turn to page 72 of her workbook.

hurries	ever	secret	puppies	tries	second	even	spies
ever	puppies	even	second	secret	spies	tries	hurries
puppies	hurries	second	tries	ever	secret	spies	even
secret	tries	puppies	second	spies	ever	even	hurries

Here are the words you copied in the last activity. Each row has the same words but in a different order. Please read all of the words as well as you can.

Your child reads the words going across each row. You may wish to place a card under the line she is reading to help her keep her place.

Correct any errors immediately.

Completing Sentences

Have your child turn to page 73 of her workbook.

Here is the page with some sentences for you to complete. Fill in the blank with the word from the two choices that makes the most sense.

Remember to say blank when you come to the blank line.

Your child should read the first sentence, saying blank when she comes to the blank line.

Your child should select the word underneath the blank line that makes the most sense and copy it on the blank line.

Have your child proceed in this way with the remaining sentences. The sentences continue on page 74.

NOTE: If your child has great difficulty with handwriting, it's fine for you yourself to write the words on the blank lines. If you do so, however, make sure that your child dictates the sounds of the word to you one at a time as you write it.

The completed sheet should look like the following figure.

1.	Tom spies on me all the time.
2.	Jill always tries to do her best.
3.	You can trust me. I can keep a secret.
4.	I can't wait another second to eat.
5.	That boy always hurries to school.
6.	Is it legal to park the care here?
7.	Sam made a lemon cake for dessert.
8.	Jill's dog just gave birth to seven puppies.
9.	The second problem was the most difficult.
10.	If Tom hurries, he can still catch his bus.

Unit Checkouts

Before moving on to the next unit, your child should be able to do the following accurately and without much hesitation:

1. Read the 8 target words in the unit easily.

2. Read the sentences presented in the Completing Sentences activity easily.

9
Unit Nine

Lesson 17

In this lesson your child will:

- sort a list of two-syllable words with the letter *i* in the first syllable depending upon what sound that letter represents
- flex nonsense words with *i*
- analyze 8 target words

Sorting Words with i

Write the letter *i* on a dry erase board or a piece of paper.

Please tell me the two common sounds for this letter.

Elicit from your child the sounds /i/ and /ie/. If she doesn't know the sounds, writes *it* and *child* on the board, underlining the *i* in each, and asks her for the sounds of the underlined letter in each word.

Have your child open her workbook to pages 76-77.

Good job! This page has a list of two-syllable words with this letter. We're going to sort them according to whether you hear /i/ or /ie/ in the first syllable of each word.

Please read the first word.

Your child reads the word. If she has difficulty reading the word, have her underline each syllable in turn and say it in isolation.

What sound do you hear in the first syllable of <u>visit</u>? /i/ or /ie/?

Your child should say /i/. If she says /ie/, tell her, "*That would make the word /viesit/*" (pronounce the first syllable *vie*), but that's not a word. If she still can't come up with the correct sound, tell it to her directly.

Let's put all the words with the /i/ sound in column 1.

Have your child say-and-write *visit* in column 1.

Repeat these steps for the remaining words:

1. Have your child read the word. If she needs to, she can underline each syllable and say it in isolation.
2. Ask, "*What sound do you hear in the first syllable of <word>? /i/ or /ie/?*"
3. Help your child identify the correct sound.
4. Have your child say-and-write words with /i/ in column 1 and words with /ie/ in column 2.

The following figure shows what the completed sorting sheet should look like.

1	2
visit	silent
pity	giant
finish	lion
river	tiger
limit	final
city	item

Flexing Practice with "i"

In this exercise your child will practice flexing nonsense words with *i*. That is, she will read them first with the /i/ sound and then with the /ie/ sound.

Have your child turn to page 78 of the her workbook.

Here are some nonsense words we will use to practice flexing.

Read each word two ways, first with the /i/ sound and then with the /ie/ sound. I'll do the first three. Listen: mi mie; pi pie; vi vie.

Run your finger under the word each time you pronounce it.

Now it's your turn to read these 3 words. Your child reads the first three words. Make sure that she first reads each word with the /i/ sound.

After your child reads these words, she should continue flexing the remaining words.

If the task is difficult for her, review one column of words intermittently throughout the day.

Breaking Words Apart

Have your child turn to page 79 of her workbook.

Follow these steps for each word:

1. Your child reads the word.

2. She copies the word neatly in her workbook.

3. She says the sounds of the word one at a time. As she says a sound, she underlines how that sound is spelled.

If your child is ever confused about how a particular sound is spelled, tell her very directly.

NOTE: The first four words on the list have two-syllables. When your child records these words, she should say the words in syllables and write each syllable on a separate line.

The following figure shows the correct markings for the words.

1.	<u>vi</u>	<u>sit</u>	5.	<u>hop</u>	
2.	<u>si</u>	<u>lent</u>	6.	<u>hope</u>	
3.	<u>gi</u>	<u>ant</u>	7.	<u>can</u>	
4.	<u>li</u>	<u>on</u>	8.	<u>cane</u>	

Lesson 18

In this lesson your child will:

- practice reading the target words for the unit
- read some multisyllable words
- complete some sentences with the target words for the unit

Word Reading Practice

Have your child turn to page 80 of her workbook.

cane	can	silent	hope	giant	visit	hop	lion
silent	visit	hop	giant	lion	can	cane	hope
lion	hop	hope	visit	cane	giant	can	silent
hop	hope	cane	can	silent	lion	visit	giant

Here are the words you copied in the last activity. Each row has the same words but in a different order. Please read all of the words as well as you can.

Your child reads the words going across each row. You may wish to place a card under the line she is reading to help her keep her place.

Correct any errors immediately.

Reading Multisyllable Words

Have your child turn to page 81 of her workbook.

Here is another list of long words for you to read. However, now that you are so good, you've got some words with 3 or 4 syllables. But your strategy remains the same one you use for 2-syllable words: Underline a syllable and say it, then do the same for the next syllable.

If your child gets stuck, help her work through the word syllable by syllable, always asking first for her to underline the next syllable and say it.

You might also have to help her flex a vowel sound if she originally tries a legitimate sound but one that isn't correct for the particular word.

Continue to practice these words in subsequent lessons until your child can read the words easily.

If your child is good at reading the individual syllables but has problems blending the syllables into whole words, you should do an oral blending warm-up before a practice session. To conduct the oral blending warm-up, say the syllables one at a time with a 1 second pause in between and have your child say the whole word. Have the workbook closed when doing this warm-up. Your child should respond just to the spoken syllables.

The following figure shows possible markings for the words. You should accept any syllable division so long as the underlined part is exactly one syllable and easy to say.

1.	<u>re</u> mem ber	5.	<u>break</u> fast	
2.	<u>prin</u> ci pal	6.	<u>no</u> bo dy	
3.	<u>be</u> yond	7.	<u>o</u> per a tion	
4.	<u>dis</u> co ver	8.	<u>im</u> por tant	

Completing Sentences

Have your child turn to page 82 of her workbook.

Here is the page with some sentences for you to complete. Fill in the blank with the word from the two choices that makes the most sense.

Remember to say <u>blank</u> when you come to the blank line.

Your child should read the first sentence, saying <u>blank</u> when she comes to the blank line.

Your child should select the word underneath the blank line that makes the most sense and copy it on the blank line.

Have your child proceed in this way with the remaining sentences. The sentences continue on page 83.

NOTE: If your child has great difficulty with handwriting, it's fine for you yourself to write the words on the blank lines. If you do so, however, make sure that your child dictates the sounds of the word to you one at a time as you write it.

The completed sheet should look like the following figure.

---

1. The class was <u>silent</u> when the teacher spoke.

2. Dad went to <u>visit</u> his grandmother.

3. Jack cut down the beanstalk to kill the <u>giant</u>.

4. The <u>lion</u> is called the king of beasts.

5. The old man needed a <u>cane</u> to help him walk.

6. Tom <u>can</u> read three books in one night.

7. I <u>hope</u> the weather tomorrow is good.

8. Jill can <u>hop</u> across the playground.

9. I went to the hospital to <u>visit</u> my sick friend.

10. That restaurant serves <u>giant</u> hamburgers.

Unit Checkouts

Before moving on to the next unit, your child should be able to do the following accurately and without much hesitation:

1. Read the 8 target words in the unit easily.

2. Read the multisyllable words in the unit easily.

3. Read the sentences presented in the Completing Sentences activity easily.

10
Unit Ten

Lesson 19

In this lesson your child will:

- sort a list of two-syllable words with the letter *o* in the first syllable depending upon what sound that letter represents
- flex nonsense words with *o*
- analyze 8 target words

Sorting Words with o

Write the letter *o* on a dry erase board or a piece of paper.

Please tell me the two common sounds for this letter.

Elicit from your child the sounds /o/ and /oa/. If she doesn't know the sounds, writes *octopus* and *go* on the board, underlining the *o* in each, and asks her for the sounds of the underlined letter in each word.

Have your child open her workbook to pages 86-87.

Good job! This page has a list of two-syllable words with this letter. We're going to sort them according to whether you hear /o/ or /oa/ in the first syllable of each word.

Please read the first word.

Your child reads the word. If she has difficulty reading the word, have her underline each syllable in turn and say it in isolation.

What sound do you hear in the first syllable of _robin_? /o/ or /oa/?

Your child should say /o/. If she says /oa/, tell her, *"That would make the word /roabin/"* (pronounce the first syllable *row*), but that's not a word. If she still can't come up with the correct sound, tell it to her directly.

Let's put all the words with the /o/ sound in column 1.

Have your child say-and-write *robin* in column 1.

Repeat these steps for the remaining words:

1. Have your child read the word. If she needs to, she can underline each syllable and say it in isolation.

2. Ask, *"What sound do you hear in the first syllable of <word>? /o/ or /oa/?"*

3. Help your child identify the correct sound.

4. Have your child say-and-write words with /o/ in column 1 and words with /oa/ in column 2.

The following figure shows what the completed sorting sheet should look like.

1	2
robin	open
copy	broken
progress	program
modern	focus
project	over
Thomas	notice

Flexing Practice with "o"

In this exercise your child will practice flexing nonsense words with *o*. That is, she will read them first with the /o/ sound and then with the /oa/ sound.

Have your child turn to page 88 of the her workbook.

Here are some nonsense words we will use to practice flexing.

Read each word two ways, first with the /o/ sound and then with the /oa/ sound. I'll do the first three. Listen: mo moa; po poa; vo voa.

Run your finger under the word each time you pronounce it.

Now it's your turn to read these 3 words. Your child reads the first three words. Make sure that she first reads each word with the /o/ sound.

After your child reads these words, she should continue flexing the remaining words.

If the task is difficult for her, review one column of words intermittently throughout the day.

Breaking Words Apart

Have your child turn to page 89 of her workbook.

Follow these steps for each word:

1. Your child reads the word.

2. She copies the word neatly in her workbook.

3. She says the sounds of the word one at a time. As she says a sound, she underlines how that sound is spelled.

If your child is ever confused about how a particular sound is spelled, tell her very directly.

NOTE: The first four words on the list have two-syllables. When your child records these words, she should say the words in syllables and write each syllable on a separate line.

The following figure shows the correct markings for the words.

1.	p r o	g r e ss	5. d o es
2.	p r o	g r a m	6. g o es
3.	p r o	j e c t	7. wh a t
4.	b r o	k e n	8. th a t

Lesson 20

In this lesson your child will:

- practice reading the target words for the unit
- read some multisyllable words
- complete some sentences with the target words for the unit

Word Reading Practice

Have your child turn to page 90 of her workbook.

progress	program	project	broken	does	goes	what
that	what	goes	progress	that	project	program
broken	does	project	that	broken	program	progress
does	goes	that	program	progress	broken	project
that	does	what	goes			

Here are the words you copied in the last activity. Each row has the same words but in a different order. Please read all of the words as well as you can.

Your child reads the words going across each row. You may wish to place a card under the line she is reading to help her keep her place.

Correct any errors immediately.

Reading Multisyllable Words

Have your child turn to page 91 of her workbook.

Here is another list of long words for you to read. To read the word, underline each syllable and say it, then blend the syllables together.

If your child gets stuck, help her work through the word syllable by syllable, always asking first for her to underline the next syllable and say it.

You might also have to help her flex a vowel sound if she originally tries a legitimate sound but one that isn't correct for the particular word.

Continue to practice these words in subsequent lessons until your child can read the words easily.

If your child is good at reading the individual syllables but has problems blending the syllables into whole words, you should do an oral blending warm-up before a practice session. To conduct the oral blending warm-up, say the syllables one at a time with a 1 second pause in between and have your child say the whole word. Have the workbook closed when doing this warm-up. Your child should respond just to the spoken syllables.

The following figure shows possible markings for the words. You should accept any syllable division so long as the underlined part is exactly one syllable and easy to say.

1. si mi lar	5. con ti nue
2. suc cess ful	6. care ful
3. ex plain	7. e ver y thing
4. in ter est ing	8. dif fer ence

Completing Sentences

Have your child turn to page 92 of her workbook.

Here is the page with some sentences for you to complete. Fill in the blank with the word from the two choices that makes the most sense.

Remember to say <u>blank</u> when you come to the blank line.

Your child should read the first sentence, saying <u>blank</u> when she comes to the blank line.

Your child should select the word underneath the blank line that makes the most sense and copy it on the blank line.

Have your child proceed in this way with the remaining sentences. The sentences continue on page 93.

NOTE: If your child has great difficulty with hand-writing, it's fine for you yourself to write the words on the blank lines. If you do so, however, make sure that your child dictates the sounds of the word to you one at a time as you write it.

The completed sheet should look like the following figure.

1.	My favorite program is on TV tonight.
2.	Dad told me that it was going to snow.
3.	I decided to throw away my broken toys.
4.	We are doing an interesting science project.
5.	Does anyone know the correct answer?
6.	Sam doesn't know what I said.
7.	Jill goes to the grocery store on Saturday.
8.	I'm making a lot of progress in my book.
9.	The high school has a good math program.
10.	I use a graph to keep track of my progress.

Unit Checkouts

Before moving on to the next unit, your child should be able to do the following accurately and without much hesitation:

1. Read the 8 target words in the unit easily.

2. Read the multisyllable words in the unit easily.

3. Read the sentences presented in the Completing Sentences activity easily.

Unit Eleven

11

Lesson 21

In this lesson your child will:

- sort a list of two-syllable words with the letter *u* in the first syllable depending upon what sound that letter represents
- flex nonsense words with *u*
- play *I Spy* and read some words with *c*
- analyze 8 target words

Sorting Words with u

Write the letter *u* on a dry erase board or a piece of paper.

Please tell me the three common sounds for this letter.

Elicit from your child the sounds /u/, /ew/ and /ue/. If she doesn't know the sounds, write *up*, *super*, and *music* on the board, underlining the *u* in each, and asks her for the sounds of the underlined letter in each word.

Have your child open her workbook to pages 96-97.

Good job! This page has a list of two-syllable words with this letter. We're going to sort them according to whether you hear /u/ /ew/ or /ue/ in the first syllable of each word. Please read the first word.

Your child reads the word. If she has difficulty reading the word, have her underline each syllable in turn and say it in isolation.

What sound do you hear in the first syllable of music? /u/, /ew/ or /ue/?

Your child should say /ue/. If she chooses a different sound, pronounce the word with that sound. If she still can't come up with the correct sound, tell it to her directly.

Let's put all the words with the /ue/ sound in column 1.

Have your child say-and-write *music* in column 1.

Repeat these steps for the remaining words:

1. Have your child read the word. If she needs to, she can underline each syllable and say it in isolation.

2. Ask, "*What sound do you hear in the first syllable of <word>? /u/, /ew/, or /ue/?*"

3. Help your child identify the correct sound.

4. Have your child say-and-write words with /ue/ in column 1, words with /ew/ in column 2, and words with /u/ in column 3.

The following figure shows what the completed sorting sheet should look like.

1	2	3
music	student	study
humid	Lucy	punish
cupid	duty	
humor	stupid	
unite		
pupil		

Flexing Practice with "u"

In this exercise, students will practice flexing nonsense words with *u*. The exercise is slightly different from the earlier flexing exercises because *u* can commonly represent not just 2 sounds, as is the case with *a, e, i,* and *o,* but 3 different sounds. To begin, students will read each syllable 2 ways, first with the /u/ sound and then with the /ew/ sound. After the students have read the entire list this way, they will go back and try to say each syllable with a /ue/ sound. In some syllables this will be easy and in some it will be difficult. Students will underline any syllable in which they can easily say /ue/.

Have your child turn to page 98 of the her workbook.

Here are some nonsense words we will use to practice flexing.

Read each word two ways, first with the /u/ sound and then with the /ew/ sound. I'll do the first three. Listen: mu mew; pu pew; vu vew.

Run your finger under the word each time you pronounce it.

Now it's your turn to read these 3 words. Your child reads the first three words. Make sure that she first reads each word with the /u/ sound.

After your child reads these words, she should continue flexing the remaining words.

If the task is difficult for her, review one column of words intermittently throughout the day.

Great job! Now let's go through the list and try to say each syllable with the /ue/ sound. Sometimes it will be easy to say and sometimes it will be hard.

If it's easy to say with the /ue/ sound, we'll underline it.

I'll do the first one. /mue/. That's pretty easy to say, so let's underline that one.

You get to do the rest.

Your child reads the remaining words with the /ue/ sound and underlines the words that are easy to say.

The following figure shows what the completed page should look like:

1.	<u>mu</u>	7.	slu
2.	<u>pu</u>	8.	gru
3.	<u>vu</u>	9.	fru
4.	tu	10.	snu
5.	<u>bu</u>	11.	pru
6.	<u>gu</u>	12.	<u>sku</u>

I Spy

Have your child turn to page 99 of her workbook.

Please write the 3 patterns where cee is /s/.

Your child writes the patterns on a dry erase board or on a separate piece of paper. Give her plenty of time to remember them. If after a minute or so she still doesn't remember any, write *ce* on the board and see if she remembers the remaining pair. If not, tell her these explicitly and have her practice intermittently throughout the lesson. (It's a good idea to have her say the letter names as she writes them.)

Now please underline any word on this list that fits the pattern.

Your child underlines the appropriate words.

Now please read all of the words.

Your child reads the words.

As necessary remind your child that in words fitting the pattern (i.e., having *ce, ci, cy*) the *c* will be pronounced /s/.

The following figure shows this page with all of the appropriate words underlined.

1.	cloth	6.	clean
2.	music	7.	copy
3.	picnic	8.	<u>city</u>
4.	public	9.	<u>dance</u>
5.	<u>place</u>	10.	<u>Nancy</u>

Breaking Words Apart

Have your child turn to page 100 of her workbook.

Follow these steps for each word:

1. Your child reads the word.

2. She copies the word neatly in her workbook.

3. She says the sounds of the word one at a time. As she says a sound, she underlines how that sound is spelled.

If your child is ever confused about how a particular sound is spelled, tell her very directly.

Notes about words

Hour and honest: Tell your child that the *h* in these words is not pronounced. She should therefore place no line under the *h*'s when marking the words and provide no sound for them. They may cover up the h when reading these words if that helps them.

Phone and graph: Write *ph* on a dry erase board or a separate piece of paper. Tell your child that these letters are used for /f/. This spelling is used at the beginning, middle, or end of a word. This digraph is used with words borrowed from the ancient Greek language.

NOTE: Five words on the list have two-syllables. When your child records these words, she should say the words in syllables and write each syllable on a separate line.

The following figure shows the correct markings for the words.

1.	<u>s</u> <u>t</u> <u>u</u>	<u>d</u> <u>e</u> <u>n</u> <u>t</u>	5.	h <u>ou</u> <u>r</u>
2.	<u>s</u> <u>t</u> <u>u</u>	<u>d</u> <u>y</u>	6.	h <u>o</u>	<u>n</u> <u>e</u> <u>s</u> <u>t</u>
3.	<u>p</u> <u>u</u>	<u>n</u> <u>i</u> <u>sh</u>	7.	<u>ph</u> <u>o</u> <u>n</u> <u>e</u>
4.	<u>m</u> <u>u</u>	<u>s</u> <u>i</u> <u>c</u>	8.	<u>g</u> <u>r</u> <u>a</u> <u>ph</u>

Lesson 22

In this lesson your child will:

- practice reading the target words for the unit
- read some multisyllable words
- complete some sentences with the target words for the unit

Word Reading Practice

Have your child turn to page 101 of her workbook.

graph	phone	study	honest	punish	student	hour	music
study	student	hour	punish	music	phone	graph	honest
music	hour	honest	student	graph	punish	phone	study
hour	honext	graph	phone	study	music	student	punish

Here are the words you copied in the last activity. Each row has the same words but in a different order. Please read all of the words as well as you can.

Your child reads the words going across each row. You may wish to place a card under the line she is reading to help her keep her place.

Correct any errors immediately.

Reading Multisyllable Words

Have your child turn to page 102 of her workbook.

Here is another list of long words for you to read. To read the word, underline each syllable and say it, then blend the syllables together.

If your child gets stuck, help her work through the word syllable by syllable, always asking first for her to underline the next syllable and say it.

You might also have to help her flex a vowel sound if she originally tries a legitimate sound but one that isn't correct for the particular word.

Continue to practice these words in subsequent lessons until your child can read the words easily.

If your child is good at reading the individual syllables but has problems blending the syllables into whole words, you should do an oral blending warm-up before a practice session. To conduct the oral blending warm-up, say the syllables one at a time with a 1 second pause in between and have your child say the whole word. Have the workbook closed when doing this warm-up. Your child should respond just to the spoken syllables.

The following figure shows possible markings for the words. You should accept any syllable division so long as the underlined part is exactly one syllable and easy to say.

1. un der stand ing	5. kan ga roo
2. in for ma tion	6. how e ver
3. lar gest	7. un der neath
4. dif fer ent	8. ma chine

Completing Sentences

Have your child turn to page 103 of her workbook.

Here is the page with some sentences for you to complete. Fill in the blank with the word from the two choices that makes the most sense.

Remember to say <u>blank</u> when you come to the blank line.

Your child should read the first sentence, saying <u>blank</u> when she comes to the blank line.

Your child should select the word underneath the blank line that makes the most sense and copy it on the blank line.

Have your child proceed in this way with the remaining sentences. The sentences continue on page 104.

NOTE: If your child has great difficulty with hand-writing, it's fine for you yourself to write the words on the blank lines. If you do so, however, make sure that your child dictates the sounds of the word to you one at a time as you write it.

The completed sheet should look like the following figure.

1.	I will study for about an <u>hour</u>.
2.	I hope you are a good <u>student</u>.
3.	Did you study the <u>graphs</u> for the math test?
4.	Did you have to <u>punish</u> the bad cat?
5.	I trust Tom because he is an <u>honest</u> person.
6.	I have to make a <u>phone</u> call now.
7.	Jill can help you <u>study</u> for the big test.
8.	Sam listens to <u>music</u> all the time.
9.	The movie is about two <u>hours</u> long.
10.	All of the <u>students</u> did their homework.

Unit Checkouts

Before moving on to the next unit, your child should be able to do the following accurately and without much hesitation:

1. Read the 8 target words in the unit easily.

2. Read the multisyllable words in the unit easily.

3. Read the sentences presented in the Completing Sentences activity easily.

ea

12
Unit Twelve

Lesson 23

In this lesson your child will:

- sort a list of words with *ea*
- analyze 8 target words

Sorting Words with ea

Write *ea* on a dry erase board or a sheet of paper. Underneath that write *sea, bread,* and *great* on a dry erase board or a piece of paper and underline the *ea* in each of the words.

Point to the *ea*.

This spelling has one main sound but it is sometimes also used for two other sounds. Please read these words and tell me the sound for the underlined part.

Have your child read the words and say the appropriate sound. If she has difficulty reading a word, tell it to her and have her repeat it.

Have your child open her workbook to pages 106 and 107.

Good job! This page has a list of words with this spelling. We're going to sort them according to whether you hear /ee/, /e/, or /ay/. Please read the first word.

Your child reads the word. If she has difficulty reading the word, tell it to her and have her repeat it.

What sound do you hear in year? /ee/, /e/, or /ay/?

Your child says /ee/.

If she says a different sound, pronounce the word with the sound that she said. If she still can't identify the correct sound, tell it to her directly and have her repeat.

Let's put all the words with the /ee/ sound in column 1.

Have your child say-and-write *year* in column 1.

Repeat these steps for the remaining words:

1. Have your child read the word. If she has difficulty reading the word, tell it to her and have her repeat.

2. Ask, "*What sound do you hear in <word>? /ee/, /e/, or /ay/?*"

3. Help your child identify the correct sound.

4. Have your child say-and-write words with /ee/ in column 1, words with /e/ in column 2, and words with /ay/ in column 3.

The following figure shows what the completed sorting sheet should look like.

1	2	3
year	bread	great
least	deaf	break
beach	head	steak
each	read	(wear)
read	(wear)	

Notes on words

Read: This word can be placed in either the /ee/ or the /e/ column depending on the form of the word that is read. Point this out to your child and have her record it in both column 1 and 2.

Wear: This word can be placed in either column 2 or column 3, depending upon which sound your child hears. The /e/ and /ay/ sounds are very similar, and the letter *r* that follows distorts the vowel sound slightly, so it is a bit different from pronunciations of the spelling not followed by *r*.

Breaking Words Apart

Have your child turn to page 108 of her workbook.

Follow these steps for each word:

1. Your child reads the word.

2. She copies the word neatly in her workbook.

3. She says the sounds of the word one at a time. As she says a sound, she underlines how that sound is spelled.

If your child is ever confused about how a particular sound is spelled, tell her very directly.

The following figure shows the correct markings for the words.

1. l ea s t	5. g r ea t
2. s c r ea m	6. b r ea k
3. b r ea d	7. w ea r
4. d ea f	8. b ea r

Lesson 24

In this lesson your child will:

- practice reading the target words for the unit
- read some multisyllable words
- complete some sentences with the target words for the unit

Word Reading Practice

Have your child turn to page 109 of her workbook.

scream	least	great	bread	deaf	wear	break	bear
deaf	great	break	least	bear	bread	wear	scream
great	break	bear	wear	scream	deaf	least	bread
break	deaf	wear	great	bread	bear	scream	least

Here are the words you copied in the last activity. Each row has the same words but in a different order. Please read all of the words as well as you can.

Your child reads the words going across each row. You may wish to place a card under the line she is reading to help her keep her place.

Correct any errors immediately.

Reading Multisyllable Words

Have your child turn to page 110 of her workbook.

Here is another list of long words for you to read. To read the word, underline each syllable and say it, then blend the syllables together.

If your child gets stuck, help her work through the word syllable by syllable, always asking first for her to underline the next syllable and say it.

You might also have to help her flex a vowel sound if she originally tries a legitimate sound but one that isn't correct for the particular word.

Continue to practice these words in subsequent lessons until your child can read the words easily.

If your child is good at reading the individual syllables but has problems blending the syllables into whole words, you should do an oral blending warm-up before a practice session. To conduct the oral blending warm-up, say the syllables one at a time with a 1 second pause in between and have your child say the whole word. Have the workbook closed when doing this warm-up. Your child should respond just to the spoken syllables.

The following figure shows possible markings for the words. You should accept any syllable division so long as the underlined part is exactly one syllable and easy to say.

1.	<u>o</u> per <u>a</u> tion	5.	move ment
2.	te le phone	6.	e du ca tion
3.	sur prise	7.	na tion al
4.	an y thing	8.	com pan y

Completing Sentences

Have your child turn to page 111 of her workbook.

Here is the page with some sentences for you to complete. Fill in the blank with the word from the two choices that makes the most sense.

Remember to say <u>blank</u> when you come to the blank line.

Your child should read the first sentence, saying <u>blank</u> when she comes to the blank line.

Your child should select the word underneath the blank line that makes the most sense and copy it on the blank line.

Have your child proceed in this way with the remaining sentences. The sentences continue on page 112.

NOTE: If your child has great difficulty with handwriting, it's fine for you yourself to write the words on the blank lines. If you do so, however, make sure that your child dictates the sounds of the word to you one at a time as you write it.

The completed sheet should look like the following figure.

1.	They did a great job making the <u>bread</u>.
2.	The secretary just went out on his <u>break</u>.
3.	I will have to study for at <u>least</u> three hours.
4.	You don't have to scream. I'm not <u>deaf</u>.
5.	We had a <u>great</u> time at the party.
6.	We saw a brown <u>bear</u> in the woods.
7.	I want to <u>wear</u> my red shirt today.
8.	The fans will <u>scream</u> when their team scores.
9.	My <u>great</u>-grandparents are from Brazil.
10.	I like to eat <u>bread</u> and jam for breakfast.

Before moving on to the next unit, your child should be able to do the following accurately and without much hesitation:

1. Read the 8 target words in the unit easily.

2. Read the multisyllable words in the unit easily.

3. Read the sentences presented in the Completing Sentences activity easily.

ou

13
Unit Thirteen

Lesson 25

In this lesson your child will:

- sort a list of words with *ou*
- analyze 8 target words
- practice reading the target words for the unit
- complete some sentences with the target words for the unit

NOTE: This unit and the remaining units are conducted in a single lesson.

Sorting Words with ou

Write *ou* on a dry erase board or a piece of paper. Underneath that write *out, you,* and *touch* and underline the *ou* in each of the words.

Point to the *ou*.

This spelling has one main sound but it is sometimes also used for two other sounds. Please read these words and tell me the sound for the underlined part.

Have your child read the words and say the appropriate sound. If she has difficulty reading a word, tell it to her and have her repeat it.

Have your child open her workbook to pages 114 and 115.

Good job! This page has a list of words with this spelling. We're going to sort them according to whether you hear /ow/, /ew/, or /u/. Please read the first word.

Your child reads the word. If she has difficulty reading the word, tell it to her and have her repeat it.

What sound do you hear in mouth? /ow/, /ew/, or /u/?

Your child says /ow/.

If she says a different sound, pronounce the word with the sound that she said. If she still can't identify the correct sound, tell it to her directly and have her repeat.

Let's put all the words with the /ow/ sound in column 1.

Have your child say-and-write *mouth* in column 1.

Repeat these steps for the remaining words:

1. Have your child read the word. If she has difficulty reading the word, tell it to her and have her repeat.

2. Ask, "*What sound do you hear in <word>? /ow/, /ew/, or /u/?*"

3. Help your child identify the correct sound.

4. Have your child say-and-write words with /ow/ in column 1, words with /ew/ in column 2, and words with /u/ in column 3.

The following figure shows what the completed sorting sheet should look like.

1	2	3
mouth	soup	enough
bounce	group	double
ground	youth	cousin
about		trouble
shout		

Breaking Words Apart

Have your child turn to page 116 of her workbook.

Follow these steps for each word:

1. Your child reads the word.

2. She copies the word neatly in her workbook.

3. She says the sounds of the word one at a time. As she says a sound, she underlines how that sound is spelled.

If your child is ever confused about how a particular sound is spelled, tell her very directly.

NOTE: Two words on the list (about and trouble) have two-syllables. When your child records these words, she should say the words in syllables and write each syllable on a separate line.

The following figure shows the correct markings for the words.

1. m <u>ou</u> th	5. g r <u>ou</u> p
2. b <u>ou</u> n ce	6. y <u>ou</u> th
3. a b <u>ou</u> t	7. y <u>ou</u> ng
4. s <u>ou</u> p	8. t r <u>ou</u> b le

Word Reading Practice

Have your child turn to page 117 of her workbook.

soup	group	youth	mouth	trouble	about	young	bounce
group	youth	trouble	young	bounce	soup	mouth	about
youth	soup	young	group	about	trouble	bounce	mouth
young	about	mouth	trouble	youth	bounce	soup	group

Here are the words you copied in the last activity. Each row has the same words but in a different order. Please read all of the words as well as you can.

Your child reads the words going across each row. You may wish to place a card under the line she is reading to help her keep her place.

Correct any errors immediately.

Completing Sentences

Have your child turn to page 118 of her workbook.

Here is the page with some sentences for you to complete. Fill in the blank with the word from the two choices that makes the most sense.

Remember to say blank when you come to the blank line.

Your child should read the first sentence, saying blank when she comes to the blank line.

Your child should select the word underneath the blank line that makes the most sense and copy it on the blank line.

Have your child proceed in this way with the remaining sentences. The sentences continue on page 119.

NOTE: If your child has great difficulty with hand-writing, it's fine for you yourself to write the words on the blank lines. If you do so, however, make sure that your child dictates the sounds of the word to you one at a time as you write it.

The completed sheet should look like the following figure.

1.	The bear opened its <u>mouth</u> and growled.
2.	The ball <u>bounced</u> off the pitcher's mound.
3.	I like to eat tomato <u>soup</u>.
4.	Please try to stay out of <u>trouble</u>.
5.	Sam belongs to an interesting youth <u>group</u>.
6.	I wrote a story <u>about</u> a lion and a mouse.
7.	I liked to ride a tricycle when I was <u>young</u>.
8.	It's no <u>trouble</u> to give you a ride home.
9.	The town has good programs for its <u>youth</u>.
10.	We're having chicken noodle <u>soup</u> for lunch.

Unit Checkouts

Before moving on to the next unit, your child should be able to do the following accurately and without much hesitation:

1. Read the 8 target words in the unit easily.

2. Read the sentences presented in the *Completing Sentences* activity easily.

ar

14

Unit Fourteen

Lesson 26

In this lesson your child will:

- sort a list of words with *ar*
- analyze 8 target words
- practice reading the target words for the unit
- complete some sentences with the target words for the unit

Sorting Words with ar

Write *ar* on a dry erase board or a piece of paper. Underneath that write *car, dollar, carry,* and *care* and underline the *ou* in each of the words.

Point to the *ar.*

This spelling has one main sound but it is sometimes also used for other sounds. Please read these words and tell me the sound for the underlined part.

Have your child read the words and say the appropriate sound. The sounds are /ar/, /er/, /a/, and /ay/, respectively.

If your child has difficulty reading a word, tell it to her and have her repeat it. When discussing the word *care*, put a loop connecting the *a* and the *e*.

care

As you have seen before, the /r/ sound distorts the vowel sound preceding it, so it doesn't sound exactly like the /ay/ in *cape*, for instance, but it is correct, nonetheless, to identify it as an /ay/ sound.

> *NOTE: One of the tricky aspects of reading words with* ar *is sometimes the spelling represents a single sound (as in* car *and* dollar*) and sometimes the* a *and the* r *each represent a sound (as in* carry *and* care*).*

Have your child open her workbook to pages 122-123.

Good job! This page has a list of words with this spelling. We're going to sort them according to whether you hear /ar/, /er/, /a/ or /ay/. Please read the first word.

Your child reads the word. If she has difficulty reading the word, tell it to her and have her repeat it.

What sound do you hear in dark? /ar/, /er/, /a/ or /ay/?

Your child says /ar/.

If she says a different sound, pronounce the word with the sound that she said. If she still can't identify the correct sound, tell it to her directly and have her repeat.

Let's put all the words with the /ar/ sound in column 1.

Have your child say-and-write *dark* in column 1.

Repeat these steps for the remaining words:

1. Have your child read the word. If she has difficulty reading the word, tell it to her and have her repeat.

2. Ask, *"What sound do you hear in <word>? /ar/, /er/, /a/, or /ay/?"*

3. Help your child identify the correct sound.

4. Have your child say-and-write words with /ar/ in column 1, words with /er/ in column 2, words with /a/ in column 3, and words with /ay/ in column 4.

The following figure shows what the completed sorting sheet should look like.

1	2	3	4
dark	dollar	carry	stare
darling		marry	share
car		parent	care
		arrow	
		carrot	

Breaking Words Apart

Have your child turn to page 124 of her workbook.

Follow these steps for each word:

1. Your child reads the word.

2. She copies the word neatly in her workbook.

3. She says the sounds of the word one at a time. As she says a sound, she underlines how that sound is spelled.

If your child is ever confused about how a particular sound is spelled, tell her very directly.

> *NOTE: Two words on the list have two-syllables, and three have three-syllables. When your child records these words, she should say the words in syllables and write each syllable on a separate line.*

The following figure shows the correct markings for the words.

1. sh ar k		5. po pu lar	
2. d ar ling		6. re gu lar	
3. ca rr o t		7. squ are	
4. pa rent		8. a re a	

Word Reading Practice

Have your child turn to page 125 of her workbook.

carrot	area	parent	darling	shark	popular	regular
square	regular	popular	shark	square	area	carrot
parent	darling	area	square	darling	regular	carrot
shark	popular	parent	darling	shark	popular	carrot
parent	square	area	regular			

Here are the words you copied in the last activity. Each row has the same words but in a different order. Please read all of the words as well as you can.

Your child reads the words going across each row. You may wish to place a card under the line she is reading to help her keep her place.

Correct any errors immediately.

Completing Sentences

Have your child turn to page 126 of her workbook.

Here is the page with some sentences for you to complete. Fill in the blank with the word from the two choices that makes the most sense.

Remember to say <u>blank</u> when you come to the blank line.

Your child should read the first sentence, saying <u>blank</u> when she comes to the blank line.

Your child should select the word underneath the blank line that makes the most sense and copy it on the blank line.

Have your child proceed in this way with the remaining sentences. The sentences continue on page 127.

NOTE: If your child has great difficulty with hand-writing, it's fine for you yourself to write the words on the blank lines. If you do so, however, make sure that your child dictates the sounds of the word to you one at a time as you write it.

The completed sheet should look like the following figure.

1.	Bugs Bunny likes to eat <u>carrots</u>.
2.	Our back yard is in the shape of a <u>square</u>.
3.	Our car uses <u>regular</u> gas.
4.	I want to read a book about <u>sharks</u>.
5.	My <u>parents</u> went to the meeting last night.
6.	That show was very <u>popular</u>.
7.	Mom always calls me her <u>darling</u>.
8.	There are a lot of new homes in that <u>area</u>.
9.	The children made dinner for their <u>parents</u>.
10.	You need to get a <u>regular</u> piece of paper.

Unit Checkouts

Before moving on to the next unit, your child should be able to do the following accurately and without much hesitation:

1. Read the 8 target words in the unit easily.

2. Read the sentences presented in the *Completing Sentences* activity easily.

ough

Unit Fifteen

15

Lesson 27

In this lesson your child will:

- sort a list of words with *ough*
- analyze 8 target words
- practice reading the target words for the unit
- complete some sentences with the target words for the unit

Sorting Words with ough

Have your child open her workbook to pages 130-131.

Write *ough* on a dry erase board or a piece of paper.

You've made it to the last sort in this workbook. Congratulations! This sort has the most complicated spelling in English, so once you've mastered it, you've made quite an accomplishment.

I'll read each word to you and then we'll figure out what sound the o-u-g-h is being used for.

NOTE: You should spell out ough using letter names in the previous sentence.

Point to the first word.

This is the word though. "Even though it is raining, I still want to play outside."

Underline the *ough* in the word in your child's workbook.

What sound for this?

Your child says /oa/.

Please say-and-write though in column 1.

Your child records the word in her workbook as directed.

Repeat these steps for the remaining words:

1. Read the word to your child and use it in a sentence.

2. Underline *ough* in the word and ask, "*What sound for this?*"

3. Help your child identify the correct sound.

4. Have your child say-and-write words with /oa/ in column 1, words with /ew/ in column 2, words with /ow/ in column 3, and words with /aw/ in column 4, words with /uf/ in column 5, and words with /off/ in column 6.

Tell your child explicitly which column the word should go in.

NOTE: When sorting enough, rough, tough, and cough, point out that the gh in these words is used for /f/. The gh does not represent a separate sound in the other ough words.

The following figure shows what the completed sorting sheet should look like.

1	2	3	4	5	6
though	through	drought	brought	enough	cough
dough			fought	rough	
			bought	tough	
			thought		

Breaking Words Apart

Have your child turn to page 132 of her workbook.

Follow these steps for each word:

1. Your child reads the word.

2. She copies the word neatly in her workbook.

3. She says the sounds of the word one at a time. As she says a sound, she underlines how that sound is spelled.

If your child is ever confused about how a particular sound is spelled, tell her very directly.

The following figure shows the correct markings for the words.

1. th ough
2. th r ough
3. d r ough t
4. b r ough t
5. e n ou gh
6. th ough t
7. d ough
8. c ou gh

Word Reading Practice

Have your child turn to page 133 of her workbook.

cough	dough	through	thought	drought	though	enough
brought	through	though	enough	brought	cough	drought
dough	thought	brought	enough	thought	though	cough
drought	dough	through	enough	thought	cough	dough
through	brought	though	drought			

Here are the words you copied in the last activity. Each row has the same words but

***in a different order. Please read all of the
words as well as you can.***

Your child reads the words going across each row. You
may wish to place a card under the line she is reading to
help her keep her place.

Correct any errors immediately.

*NOTE: This group of words is very difficult to read
in an isolated word list such as this. If your child struggles
at all, focus on learning just 2 or 3 of the words at a time.
The most difficult challenge is to distinguish among through,
thought, and though because they are spelled so similarly. It
is a good idea to present these three together after your child
has learned the other five words.*

Completing Sentences

Have your child turn to page 134 of her workbook.

***Here is the page with some sentences for you
to complete. Fill in the blank with the word
from the two choices that makes the most
sense.***

***Remember to say <u>blank</u> when you come to
the blank line.***

Your child should read the first sentence, saying <u>blank</u>
when she comes to the blank line.

Your child should select the word underneath the blank
line that makes the most sense and copy it on the blank line.

Have your child proceed in this way with the remaining
sentences. The sentences continue on page 135.

*NOTE: If your child has great difficulty with hand-
writing, it's fine for you yourself to write the words on the
blank lines. If you do so, however, make sure that your child
dictates the sounds of the word to you one at a time as you
write it.*

The completed sheet should look like the following
figure.

---

1. I'm not <u>through</u> with my dinner yet.

2. I think I've studied <u>enough</u> for the test.

3. I caught a cold and also had a bad <u>cough</u>.

4. The sea was <u>rough</u> and choppy.

5. We <u>brought</u> a cake to the party.

6. I <u>thought</u> Sam would be here by now.

7. You should not drive <u>through</u> a red light.

8. I <u>bought</u> a new toy yesterday.

9. Mom <u>thought</u> we would like some cookies.

10. Tom <u>brought</u> his dog to school.

Unit Checkouts

Before moving on to the next unit, your child should
be able to do the following accurately and without much
hesitation:

1. Read the 8 target words in the unit easily.

2. Read the sentences presented in the *Completing
Sentences* activity easily.